An Update Luxemburg Economics'

or

Economics is Still a Peculiar Science?

Phillip Sutton

Figure 1, Rosa Luxemburg speaking at a meeting in Stuttgart in 1907 [1]

Contents

Introduction

When I wrote 'Wages, Prices and Profit in the 21st Century'[2] I referenced 'What is Economics'[3] by Rosa Luxemburg as one of the most important books that help us understand capitalism.   It explains the features of class society and why economics is a subject specific to capitalism and in this way demonstrates Marx's approach to understanding history by illustrating just how the structures and social ideas that exist in different societies are a product of the needs of the ruling class of the time.   These are very important concepts that remain essential to understanding the world today.

This all remains true, but what I didn't realise at the time of writing is that 'What is Economics' is only a section of the material that was found for this book after her death. In fact there is a much longer version prepared by Paul Levi in 1925 under the title 'Introduction to Political Economics'[4] and even this version is not the whole book as various parts were lost when Luxemburg died. The writings we still have though bear witness to the depth of Luxemburg's understanding of economic history. However, unless you are a history student, this depth of knowledge is also its downfall at least for those still getting to grips with working class politics.   It has just got too much detail on the history of pre-capitalist societies so in the end I would still recommend 'What is Economics' as a clearer document.

Luxemburg's book in whatever form is now more than a century old but I still think its quality and strength make it worthwhile revisiting the contents and relating them to what has happened in society since Luxemburg wrote the original.

I will therefore follow the framework of ideas that Luxemburg tackled in the version entitled 'What is Economics' but focus on bringing out the most important ideas and their relevance to today's world. She compares feudalism and slave society with capitalism and identifies the class structure of each and thereby gives practical evidence as to Marx's historical materialism.   What she does not do however is provide a direct explanation of the theory of historical materialism which I do think is a useful supplement to include here. A topic she could not address fully at the time is the decline of capitalism as she lived in the period in which capitalism was only just completing its ascendant period.   With over a century of hindsight, it is possible now to extend her work with a view of how capitalism has developed since the start of the 20th century and explain issues relating to the alternatives of socialism or barbarism in greater depth than she did. In this respect I have tackled the alternatives of socialism and barbarism which Luxemburg certainly saw as the two possible outcomes for the end of capitalism. As forecasts their actual meanings as forecasts remain open to interpretation and

2   Sutton P, 2020, *Wages Price and Profit in the 21st Century*
    https://www.amazon.co.uk/Wages-Price-Profit-21st-Century-ebook/dp/B089FJCPYF/
    ref=sr_1_4dchild=1&keywords=wages+price+and+profit&qid=1599516563&sr=8-4
3   Luxemburg, What is Economics in Mary Alice Walters 1970 *Rosa Luxemburg Speaks*
    Pathfinder Press
4   Luxemburg, 1925, Introduction to Political Economics in Hudis P (ed.) (2013) *The Complete Works of Rosa Luxemburg*, Volume I: Economic Writings I. London: Verso Books

I have tried to explain and pose questions about them in the context of where we have got to in the 21st Century.

In Appendix 1 I have included what is said to be Luxemburg's own plan for her book.

To be honest though I did not realise just how broad a scope this would have and just how many topics would have to be touched on in my booklet. I have tried to keep the focus sharp and I'm afraid there are many issues mentioned on which this booklet has not been able to expand and I hope the reader will bear this in mind and excuse me.

Be happy then, despite the title this is not a study of economics as such. It is a booklet about social history, about social and political change, about social and economic organisation and about class society. Luxemburg's book was a critique of economics and of capitalist society and that is what you must expect from my booklet too.

A Brief Biography

Rosa Luxemburg, born Rozalie Luxenburg in Poland in 1871, was active in socialist organisations as a teenager even before she went to Zurich to study in 1889. She specialised in politics, economics and the middle ages and completed a doctorate with a dissertation on the industrial development of Poland. She moved to Germany in 1897 to continue militant campaigning for a socialism revolution and in Germany she taught economics at the German Social Democratic Party (SDP) school in Berlin. 'What is Economics' was based on her lecturing materials which she had collected over the period she was teaching. However she was not known primarily as an economics specialist. She was a leading public figure in the revolutionary wing of social democracy (there was such a thing in those days) and, as well as being a dynamic public speaker, she was also a leading theoretician of the revolutionary movement during this time. She was an influential figure in the development of the internationalist wing of the workers movement in Germany and produced many important theoretical writings which remain a guide for those who seek to end capitalism today and replace it with a socialist society. When WW1 broke out she rejected the support the German Social Democratic Party (SDP) gave to the war and soon joined with Karl Liebknecht to form a radical revolutionary group, the Spartakists. She continued to be a leading figure in fight against the reformist politics that had taken hold of the SDP especially after if voted to support Germany in WW1. During the German Revolution in 1918/19 she continued to support the revolutionary confrontations of the working class with the old German state and its allies the SPD. Along with Karl Liebknecht, Rosa Luxemburg was murdered in January 1919 by the Freikorps, an army of ultra nationalist ex-military who were let loose on the German revolution in by the German Social Democratic Party. The latter actively sought to prevent the workers and soldiers councils that had been set up across Germany from taking power because it was intent on being the new government itself.

A fuller autobiography[5] is available at https://rosalux.nyc/rosa-remix/.

---

5   Rosa Luxemburg Stiftung, 2016, *Rosa Remix* RLS New York

Prison Photo from Warsaw Citadel ca 1906 [6]

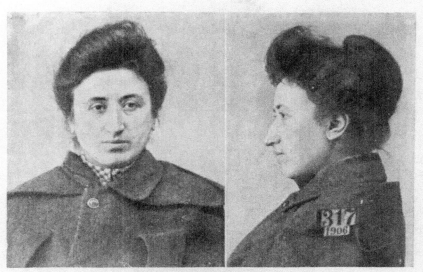

ROSA LUXEMBOURG
(Fiche anthropométrique de la prison de Varsovie)

6   rosaluxemburgblog, available at
     https://rosaluxemburgblog.files.wordpress.com/2015/09/1906-rosa-luxemburg-in-warsaw-prison-iisg-high-res.jpg accessed 1.2.21

So What is Economics Anyway?

The best place to start is with a quote from Rosa Luxemburg herself, in fact the very first paragraph of 'What is Economics'.

> Economics is a peculiar science. Problems and controversies arise as soon as we take the first step in this field of knowledge, as soon as the fundamental question - what is the subject matter of this science - is posed. The ordinary working man, who has only a very vague idea of what economics deals with, will attribute his haziness on this particular point to a shortcoming in his general education. Yet, in a certain sense, he shares his perplexity with many learned scholars and professors who write multi-volumed works dealing with the subject of economics and who teach courses in economics to college students. It appears incredible, and yet it is true, that most professors of economics have a very nebulous idea of the actual subject matter of their erudition. [7]

That sets the tone clearly doesn't it.

Luxemburg's criticism of the professors of economics of her time was not that she didn't understand what they said, she understood them very well and knew they were talking rubbish. She demonstrated that what they were saying was some variant of the idea that economics is about the economy. Not a very clever solution!

Does this still hold true today though? Surely with a hundred years more experience economists have come up with something clearer?

There are now 2 ways for us to look at economics, one is through the theory and the other is the real world events and the involvement of modern economic thinking in them.

Modern Economic Theory

To look at 21st Century economic theory, a good starting point is to investigate what modern economics is actual being taught in schools on the assumption that this is the basic theory on which the economics professors and governmental advisors base their guidance for economies in the real world. After all we would expect that from the mathematics, physics, biology and other sciences that schools teach, wouldn't we!

---

7   Luxemburg, What is Economics in Mary Alice Walters 1970 *Rosa Luxemburg Speaks* Pathfinder Press

By taking A level courses (see 'A level Economics'[8]) as a sample therefore, the main observation to be made is that there is very little actual theory present. The majority of the content is simply observational. It is about the identification of situations and of different types of institutions and businesses, and descriptions of the practices of these institutions and businesses. Now we should not diminish this aspect of learning as its important to know what actually happens in the real world for those that still have to work in it. A-level Economics and Business Studies can be a good contribution for administrative workers preparing for employment.

However, in terms of theory ie an actual analysis of why things happen in the commercial world, it makes grim reading. There is little attempt at all to explain what economics is and its history, and nothing more theoretical than perfect competition, supply and demand, and so-called laws of comparative and absolute advantage. If you don't know what these are, don't go rushing off to study them, they will be explained briefly but they are clearly very superficial and frankly they are of little help if you are trying to truly understand what makes the real world tick.

Perfect competition is so unreal that it is absurd. Perfect competition is supposed to be a model for how competition works in the marketplace. It is based on the idea that a perfect market is where competition works best because there are lots of sellers, lots of customers, customers having perfect knowledge about the marketplace, and all prices being the same. For a model or abstraction like this to be useful it has to reflect reality by simplifying it and it has to describe and explain what is true or tends to be true. The nearest example to perfect competition is probably a basic peasant economy and this certainly is not the structure of capitalist markets today and nor are they moving towards such a structure. So not only has perfect competition never actually existed, it never ever will either!

The idea of supply and demand is based on the assumption that perfect competition works[9] which is not a good start. Although it can explain some adjustments in exchange prices, it just does not set standard market prices despite what these books say. Supply and demand is simply an attempt to explain price by the volumes of buying and selling taking place but it cannot do this because whilst buying and selling can create profits for individual capitalists, for capitalism as a whole, it creates nothing new and can only shift value around. Only labour can create value and prices are established dependent on the amount of waged labour contained in each product[10]. Furthermore, as Hill and Myatt[11] argue, supply curves do not work at all in imperfectly competitive markets which is of course what all markets are nowadays anyway.

Absolute and comparative advantage relate to the benefits to be obtained from international trade. Absolute advantage is no law whatsoever because it just says you can make money if you have an advantage over other suppliers – mmm

8   CGP Books, 2015, *A level Economics – Complete Revision Guide*, CGP
9   Hill & Myatt, 2010, *The Economics Anti-Textbook*, Fernwood Publishing
10   Sutton P, 2020, *Wages Price and Profit in the 21st Century*,
     https://www.amazon.co.uk/Wages-Price-Profit-21st-Century-ebook/dp/B089FJCPYF/
     ref=sr_1_4dchild=1&keywords=wages+price+and+profit&qid=1599516563&sr=8-4
11   Hill & Myatt, 2010, *The Economics Anti-Textbook*, Fernwood Publishing

clever!! Comparative advantage is, on the other hand, just plain deception. It suggests 2 countries, when they trade with each other, should specialise in the goods they are best at producing and thereby both countries can make profits from the trade. Tell that to the countries of Africa, Asia and Central America who produce cash crops for the powerful trading nations and yet have not been able to develop into healthy economies. African GDP grows at a far lower rate[12] than the European, American or Chinese economies despite or more likely because of all the foreign investment in Africa. It's true that some countries in Asia have been able to develop strong economies over the past few decades but that has been a result primarily of offering cheap labour to global markets and by gaining high levels of investment in production facilities from wealthy countries.

Economic Policy in Practice

Another way of looking at economic theory and judging economics is to look what the politicians and professors of economists have achieved in the world especially as they have become more influential during the past century as a consequence of the state playing a bigger role in the management of national economies.

Do we detect order and understanding or even control? No of course we don't, economists are as puzzled today as they were 100 years ago.

Nobody managed to solve the economic problems after World War 1, in fact the crash of 1927 came as a total surprise and was followed by a decade of unemployment and poverty leading to .... another world war! This was the only solution the politicians could come up with after the economists failed to find a way to treat the post-war problems. Let's knock it all down and start again. Wonderful!

It would be wrong to say that the politicians and economists cannot learn however. After WW2 a very different set of economic policies which emphasised mutual support and international cooperation by nation states were implemented. Well, that is as long as they cooperated with either the USA or the USSR who dominated the 2 blocs of nations in this period. This approach to reconstruction was vastly different to what happened after WW1 when the victors were far more interested in extracting financial restitution than rebuilding and, to be honest, vastly more successful. The period after WW2 saw cooperation and support for the defeated nations and led to the USA's Marshall Plan to rebuild Europe and control Germany as well as international organisations like the early forms of the European Union, the Council of Europe, the United Nations, the World Trade Organisation, Organisation for Economic Cooperation and Development, International Criminal Court and the G20. On the Russian side, the trading bloc COMECON was founded and 5 Year Plans or similar were established for managing this bloc of nations although, as the weaker economic bloc, its focus was more on developing its military capacity to compete with the USA bloc.

In fact, the economic theories that supported this change were down particularly to a man called John Maynard Keynes who established his own branch of

---

12   Our World in Data, *Economic Growth*, available at
     https://ourworldindata.org/economic-growth, accessed on 25.1.21

economics known as Keynesianism. This comprised of demand management policies that were based on high taxation and government spending to provide a stimulus to national economies. This policy approach also led to state ownership of industry as a way of managing the growth process.

Learning may have taken place but it wasn't a lasting solution. It didn't solve the economic problems faced by capitalism.

Absolute proof that this temporary growth did not mean that the professors could not control the economy came by the 1960s when the growth rates were declining and suddenly industries were collapsing, unemployment was growing, and interest rates and inflation were ridiculously high. The professors were once again floundering and so Keynesian policies were dropped and what were called monetary policies took their place. Led by professors like Milton Friedman and implemented by politicians like Margaret Thatcher in the UK, these policies imposed austerity on the world population. Thatcher was a forthright politician who pushed these policies in the UK but they were taken up in most of the world's nations by both left or right wing governments. It was simply that the old policies were clearly no longer working so they had to find a new approach. Monetary policy focused on austerity by controlling wages and limiting the availability of money with the target of reducing inflation and debt. It also emphasised private enterprise and the denationalisation and deregulation of industries and services.

Sounds good doesn't it – balance the budget and let industry flower, its just common sense really! Unfortunately after being successful for a while in reducing inflation and interest rates, these policies also came to create new problems and brought about new crises at the start of the 21st century.

Greed had taken over and the CEOs running private industries became fat-cats earning fortunes whether their firms made profits or not. The financial institutions found themselves awash with money as the wealthy realised they could make more money by playing the stock markets than by investing in productive industry. Still in 2020 the rich are continuing to get richer as they earn ever greater percentages of global wealth and, of course, the poor get poorer.

The benefits of financial investment themselves became a problem in this period as the belief spread that money could be made from riskier and riskier investments. Eventually, in 2008, we saw a collapse of financial businesses in America that had a knock-on effect across the world. Banks needed support and governments ran up major debts to protect them. Debt levels skyrocketed and the belt of austerity was tightened once again with the target again being to balance the books of the national economies.

Austerity was therefore the main focus again for the next few years (with the working class suffering most of course) until 2020 when the monetary policies were dropped in the face of the coronavirus pandemic. Suddenly governments now found the ability to build up enormous debts in order to prevent the collapse of economies - austerity was forgotten.

In the UK, one interesting feature of the right wing policies at the start of the 21st century had been the call for less government on the basis that the UK dominated the world in the 19th century when there was little state influence over the economy, so it is argued that if the role of government is reduced, the UK economy will flourish once again. It could be as simple as that, just turn back time! What's more this was a policy that spread across the world. Milton Friedman was one of the professors who pushed this line partly because he presenting it as a political viewpoint and held that such policies would support democratic systems and increase freedom as well as benefit capitalists. This seems to demonstrate the lack of new ideas that the ruling class and their advisors, the professors, can come up with nowadays.

This brief history demonstrates the lack of success achieved by governments in the management of the economy over the 20th and 21st centuries. The professors just have not been able to demonstrate any ability to find lasting solutions let alone actual cures to the problems that emerge. In fact what becomes clear is that the professors are still really in the same position as Luxemburg said back at the start of the 20th century:

> What is noteworthy in all this is the fact that the crisis is looked up and treated by all concerned, but all of society, as something beyond the sphere of human volition and beyond human control, as a heavy blow struck by an invisible and greater power, an ordeal sent down from the heavens, similar to a heavy thunderstorm, an earthquake, or a flood." [13]

The early economists like Ricardo, Say, Adam Smith and others were actual theoreticians even if they didn't come up with complete answers. They tried to analyse how the new capitalist system was working, how it created value and social wealth and benefited mankind. Marx started with their analyses and developed them into a theory that really could explain how capitalism worked and created value. Since then, it is not entirely humorous to suggest that economists (and social scientists) have studied their subjects in the hope of disproving Marx's ideas. Their analyses however have remained superficial because their aim has been primarily to support and improve the functioning of capitalism

Alfred Marshall, an important economist at the end of the 19th century, was quoted by Luxemburg as saying:

> Political Economy or Economics is a study of mankind in the ordinary business of life; it examines that part of individual and social action which is most closely connected with the attainment and with the use of the material requisites of wellbeing. [14]

One of the more important academics of the mid 20th century, Lionel Robbins, explained in 'An Essay on the Nature and Significance of Economic Science':

---

13 Luxemburg, What is Economics in Mary Alice Walters 1970 *Rosa Luxemburg Speaks* Pathfinder Press p 232
14 Luxemburg, What is Economics in Mary Alice Walters 1970 *Rosa Luxemburg Speaks* Pathfinder Press p 232

Economics is the science which studies human behaviour as a relationship between given ends and scarce means which have alternative uses. [15]

What does it tell you anything though about money and markets and value and profits? Is it any different to social sciences for example? Today, the Oxford Dictionary actually is a bit better but it also misses the one important connection which we will come back to soon.

Economics is - the study of how a society organizes its money, trade, and industry. [16]

Returning to Milton Freedman's views as he has had a major influence on governmental policies during the 2nd half of the 20th century. He clearly linked his economic policies to the idea that a reduction in state power would strengthen the economy as well as democracy and freedom.

The free man will ask neither what his country can do for him, nor what he for his country. He will ask rather "What can I and my compatriots do through government" to help us discharge our individual responsibilities to achieve our several goals and purposes, and above all, to protect our freedom? And he will accompany this question with another: "How can we keep the government from becoming a Frankenstein that will destroy the very freedom we establish it to protect?" Freedom is a rare and delicate plant. Our minds tell us, and history confirms, that the great threat to freedom is concentration of power. [17]

Thomas Piketty[18] has created a stir in recent years through his investigations of the world economy and in particular of the income disparities in the system. As a left leaning economist, he of course suggests that capitalism will actually work better if these income disparities are reduced by state intervention globally.

The definitions of economics have therefore have improved little but they have seemed to vary somewhat and take in new emphases from logistics, resources, decision-making to culture depending on the period[19].

Have you ever noticed how politicians of left and right have very different economic theories that funnily enough tend to support the policies of left and right

---

15   economicconcepts.com, *Robbins Definition of Economics, available at https://economicsconcepts.com/economics_as_a_science_of_scarcity_and_choice.htm accessed on 1.2.21*

16   Oxford Dictionary online, 2020, available at https://www.oxfordlearnersdictionaries.com/definition/english/economics accessed on 2.1.21

17   Friedman M, 1962, *Capitalism and Freedom,* https://quotepark.com/quotes/1939756-milton-friedman-the-free-man-will-ask-neither-what-his-country-can/ accessed on 1.2.21

18   Piketty T, 2020, *Capital and Ideology,* Harvard Uni Press

19   See Appendix 3

wing governments? One wonders what came first, the politics or the economics. It was probably the politics, but either way, so much for a science!

What has changed significantly since Luxemburg's time is the number of so-called expert economists and the number of books they have written. What they have come up with is not an explanation of how capitalism works but a focus on superficial elements of the economy that can be adjusted to suit the needs of one or other section of the ruling class. These investigations of supply and demand, comparative and absolute advantage, mutual advantage, perfect and imperfect competition, monopoly and oligopoly, macro and micro economics, economic cycles, inflation and deflation, globalisation, protectionism, free trade, economies of scale, free trade areas & customs unions and political unions just do not analyse the hows or whys.

> The problem with the idea that economics is purely or even primarily a descriptive undertaking is that the apparatus of economic has been shaped by an agenda focused on showing that markets are good for people rather than on discovering how markets actually work. [20]

In other words, economics theory is biased and not genuinely analytical.

Interestingly there has also been an increase in suspicion about economics and the economists of the past century given their miserable history of understanding and managing the economy. 'Anti-economics' has become a thing which says it is radical but which still avoids understanding Marx and just does not attempt to develop into a critique of capitalism. What it does is question the assumptions of textbook economics and in particular the assumption of impartiality by the professors and the approach that always blames peripheral issues for causing problems rather than the theory itself.

> The authors (of economics textbooks) seem to be unaware that it is impossible for any social science, or any individual researcher, to avoid adopting some world-view. [21]

> So the emphasis on competitive markets imparts a market fundamentalist bias to the standard textbook – it is biased against government intervention and government regulation' [22]

These critiques of economics are no more than criticisms of elements of mainstream or classical economics. They do not aim to '... discourage anyone from studying economics"[23]. They seem to perform the role of a loyal opposition.

There is an argument to say that economics today is actually worse than in Marx's and Luxemburg's time precisely because it has become an ideological tool for the ruling class. Classical economists such as Ricardo Say and Adam Smith were at

20   Marglin, 2008, quoted in Hill and Myatt 2010 *The Anti Economics Text Book*, Zed Books
21   Hill and Myatt, 2010, *The Anti Economics Text Book*, Zed Books
22   ibid
23   ibid

very least trying to analyse the real world and why things happened and, as Hill and Myatt clearly pose, there is even less questioning of existing theories or proposing of alternative theories.

> Indeed 'economics' has come to be synonymous with the economics of a particular view of capitalism. It was not always that way. At one time, economic textbooks routinely contained chapters on alternative economic systems... [24]

In many ways, we could say Adam Smith had a more honest definition of economics despite Luxemburg's overall criticisms as he simply said that economics is a study or science of wealth.

> The great object of Political Economy of every country is to increase the riches and power of that country. [25]

Finally there is another group of economics professors which are worth our attention – the so-called marxist economists. These base themselves on Marx's theory of waged labour, surplus value and commodity production BUT as academics their problem is that they exist to advise governments, politicians and businesspeople, they are not part of a workers' movement that seeks to revolutionise society. They ignore the idea that Marx was critical of economics and wanted to get rid of it, they ignore the idea there is no such thing as marxist economics policies.

Some do use Marx's idea more clearly than others of course so let's look at one interesting example in Dr Richard Wolff, who produced this very instructive Youtube interview [26]. In the first half of the video he explains very clearly in down to earth language the state of play of capitalism today and the problems it faces and even addresses the socialism or barbarism alternatives that are discussed later in this booklet. He says he is a marxist and explains wage labour and surplus value very clearly. However it gradually turns out that he believes that socialism is represented by the likes of Bernie Sanders and that all we need is to democratise the workplace and share out the wealth among the people. He rejects religion because it is idealist but then comes up with this idealistic nonsense himself. Wolff also defends the USSR as socialist experiment that failed so he is basically defending state capitalism and pretending that is socialism, he is defending fake socialists and fake socialism. So much for an understanding of Marx!

Another example is of a marxist professor is Michael Roberts and again there is a Youtube video [27] that demonstrates a clarity in understanding the increasing problems that capitalism is facing but he also demonstrates this academic

---

24   ibid
25   Adam Smith, 1776, *The Wealth of Nations* avaiable at
      https://www.marxists.org/reference/archive/smith-adam/works/wealth-of-nations/
      book02/ch05.htm Book 2 Chapter 5
26   Wolff R, 2016, Marxism 101: *How Capitalism is Killing Itself* ,
      https://www.youtube.com/watch?
      v=6P97r9Ci5Kg&fbclid=IwAR3zexFOQDF3xQZ5qsTYHU8vVZw0TEAtoeKopEdwhiuv
      W8OQgpuYFPsV9Hgrichard+Wolff accessed 1.2.21

approach that leads to recommendations for how to improve capitalism rather than get rid of it. Clearly not a marxist!

What all of the above-mentioned have quite failed to understand or even wanted to understand is what Marx and Luxemburg amongst many other real socialists have been explaining for over a century.

Economics is quite simple the study of the capitalist relations of production and its dependence on the anarchy of the market.

So, yes of course, capitalism and its markets are affected by factors in society such as logistics, scarcity, distribution, environment, culture just as the professors try to explain but these factors are in reality just too innumerable to mention and too many to allow a single neat analysis that helps capitalism. That the market is anarchic is the only valid explanation.

Figure 2 How The Economy Works [28]

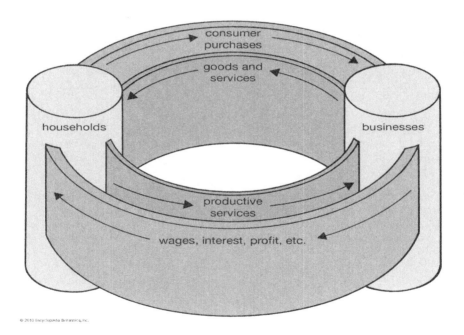

© 2010 Encyclopædia Britannica, Inc.

27   Roberts M, 2020, *Covid and The Challenges to Capitalism,*
     https://www.youtube.com/watch?
     v=cEF8LDO5Y5A&feature=youtu.be&fbclid=IwAR0R3SueCxPZAn8wV69GUTo7X-
     jz6W1jnjM4ldgovBtMWwm-ZYA3IVc5lX8h accessed 1.2.21
28   Encyclopedia Britannica, *Economics,* available at
     https:www.britannica.com/topic/economics accessed on 1.2.21

Just look at this simple diagram of how economics works in today's society. It is interesting because it displays in a very simple way the complexity of the market relationships in capitalism. There is no planning here, no ultimate control over any of these processes, it is all left to the market. Clearly, this diagram bears absolutely no relation to the processes involved in slave or feudal society as you will see in the next chapter.

If this represents the core processes of capitalist relations, then it must be recognised that everything that goes on in the world affects this process. No wonder there is no theory in economics to explain it all!

Economics, as a subject for investigation, just did not exist within slave or feudal society let alone primitive communism, in fact, the so-called science of economics only came into existence as capitalism developed, (Adam Smith's The Wealth of Nations, was published in 1776, less than 150 years before Luxemburg was writing). As pointed out by Luxemburg, this fact is ignored by the professors who just cannot link economics to capitalism and the relationships it has created.

> It should be clear by now why the bourgeois economists find it impossible to point out the essence of their science, to put the finger on the gaping wound in the social organism, to denounce its innate infirmity. To recognise and acknowledge that anarchy is the vital motive force of the rule of capital is to pronounce its death sentence in the same breath, to assert that its days are numbered.
> [29]

The learned professors cannot provide a competent definition of economics because they are too involved in supporting capitalist society. Only socialists can understand economics for what it actually is because they stand outside the system and critically analyse.

> … it is precisely this anarchy which is responsible fo the fact the economy of human society produces results which are mysterious and unpredictable to the people involved. Its anarchy is what make the economic life of mankind something unknown alien uncontrollable. [30]

Business Management Theory

In the 19th Century there was a period of scientific discovery when individuals took on the tasks of investigating and developing new sciences and areas of study and this included the issue of economics and how value is created. However, one field of study that did not emerge until the 20th century and which would support and extend the early ideas about the economy, was the field of business and

---

[29] Luxemburg, What is Economics in Mary Alice Walters 1970 *Rosa Luxemburg Speaks* Pathfinder Press p238

[30] Ibid p238

management studies. Business practice and management techniques were something that Luxemburg had little opportunity to investigate. These new areas of study emerged in consequence of the difficult problems faced by capitalist society in the 20th century.

By the 20th century large scale factory production had come to dominate instead of small craft units. Wars, revolutions and periodic increases in class struggle, increased competition between individual firms and between nations, falling profitability and the need to extract greater profits from labour have all been important features of economic and political life in this period. There emerged the necessity to control the working class as well as increase exploitation so that the system could be more efficient and profits could be maintained.

About the start of the century, FW Taylor was studying work practice and started to investigate how time and motion study could improve efficiency in production. Shortly afterwards, Henry Ford was also improving production line process (he wasn't the originator despite production line techniques becoming known as Fordism) but the specialisation of tasks required for this was complemented well by Taylor's time and motion studies. Taylor was also responsible for the radical idea that paying wages motivates workers! Perhaps we should not laugh at this idea, remembering that in recent years we have seen the emergence of unpaid internships, zero hours contracts and the increased use of immigrant labour in conditions of slavery.

As market competition intensified in the following period, the focus on marketing techniques grew as a way of selling the products being made and thereby outselling rivals. Whilst this would have benefits for individual firms through spreading knowledge about products in the markets, this only enhanced competition of course. As a result, marketing became far more than simple advertising and eventually marketing departments gained a significant role in all firms, even to the extent of designing products so that they would sell better.

Towards the end of the century, another development was that quality systems became more than just end-of-line checks. Quality became 'customer focused' and grew into systems that linked not just increased efficiencies in production but also gave workers the extra task of managing quality control themselves. This was the development of Total Quality Management (TQM) and its later version QMS (Quality Management Systems). These practical stages were accompanied by further investigations into motivation of workers, more efficient production practices that reduced material usage and environmental damage and reduced stock costs (just-in-time supply), health and safety practice became a matter of law in many countries and not forgetting the control and supervision of workers using the IT equipment itself. With all these developments, human resource management and marketing systems have basically become secondary to quality management in the organisation of the modern firm.

At the end of the century, electronics and automation further changed working practices significantly through improved efficiency in all types of organisation and not least by facilitating the global expansion of firms and industries. Computerisation significantly reduced manual administrative work and eliminated the need for vast rooms of office equipment and storage space. Electronic control and communication systems meant that production systems could be modified more quickly. Smaller firms and the subcontracting of manufacture grew in importance as they could adapt to the rapid changes more easily yet remain under central control. Communication systems between people and computers improved enormously and alongside all this transportation became much cheaper.

These issues are not the focus of this booklet but they are relevant to understanding how capitalism has changed during the 20th Century to help businesses compete in the global economy. These changes in management practice came about to suit the needs of the ruling class as the pressures on economic and business conditions changed and as the need to extract ever more profit from workers persisted.

Historical Materialism

'What is Economics' describes the links between events and their historical context but it does that without really explaining Marx's very perceptive theory about how human society has developed, ie 'Historical Materialism' or 'the Materialist Conception of History'.

We will therefore look at Luxemburg had to say about the Middle Ages (and do please read Luxemburg's original) but this chapter will start by explaining in a bit more detail what the theory of historical materialism says.

Capitalism has been very clever over the past century in persuading us that all history has been one continuous buildup to society as we know it today, that we have the most civilised society and that capitalism is normal or natural. This is simply self-justification and even self-preservation. It is an attempt to pull wool over our eyes. To understand this it is necessary to investigate more specifically Marx's view of history.

There are 2 key elements of historical materialism to recognise; the mode or method of production in existence and the class structure that corresponds to it.

Marx identified that the mode of production[31], the organisation by which life and its reproduction is supported, was the basis of any given society and set the foundations for how people behaved and thought.

> The mode of production of material life conditions the general process of social, political and intellectual life. It is not the consciousness of men that determines their existence, but their social existence that determines their consciousness. [32]

Marx also summarised this in a different way by saying that history is made by men but not in conditions of their own choosing. That is, the material conditions we are born into set our ideas and behaviours. So, for example, the tribal communities of North American were originally nomadic hunter-gatherers although, as a product of the different geographies in the continent, they gradually took up differing lifestyles and some became agricultural and lived in more permanent villages. Until the colonialists let loose by capitalism began to destroy them, these societies all remained tribal and communal, and their beliefs and behaviours reflected their lifestyles:

---

31 The mode (or method) of production is a broad definition of how a specific society is organised to produce the means of subsistence for life in that society. The means of production or the productive forces are the machinery or equipment used, the tools and raw materials, the class of workers and the technology that exists.

32 Marx, 1859, *Preface to A Contribution to the Critique of Political Economy* available at https://www.marxists.org/archive/marx/works/1859/critique-pol-economy/preface.htm accessed on 1.2.21

Before our white brothers came to civilize us we had no jails. Therefore we had no criminals. You can't have criminals without a jail. We had no locks or keys, and so we had no thieves. If a man was so poor that he had no horse, tipi or blanket, someone gave him these things. We were too uncivilized to set much value on personal belongings. We wanted to have things only in order to give them away. We had no money, and therefore a man's worth couldn't be measured by it. We had no written law, no attorneys or politicians, therefore we couldn't cheat. We really were in a bad way before the white men came, and I don't know how we managed to get along without these basic things which, we are told, are absolutely necessary to make a civilized society. [33]

In this instance, their ideas and beliefs were based on a tribal lifestyle but whilst there had been gradual changes in this lifestyle but it was too slow and as with other aboriginal communities across the world, the confrontation with an external force, ie capitalist colonialism, brought about an abrupt and violent end. In Europe however, tribal society had been replaced firstly by slave society and then by feudal society and this had been brought about by gradual technical changes and internal conflicts which had led to an internal social development never achieved by aboriginal communities. By the time capitalism emerged, a dynamic and aggressive society had been created which believed itself to be superior and which imposed itself on the rest of the world.

All of these societies generated new material conditions on which base new sets of beliefs and ideas were produced which justified tribal sharing, slave holding, the rights of domination by kings and queens, and finally the superiority of private property and the market economy and these gradual changes enabled society and history to move forward[34]. Please note that by the term 'material conditions' we mean the combination of the physical world and the social existence of humanity at that time ie human knowledge, behaviours and beliefs.

The materialist conception of history starts from the proposition that the production of the means to support human life and, next to production, the exchange of things produced, is the basis of all social structure; that in every society that has appeared in history, the manner in which wealth is distributed and society divided into classes or orders is dependent upon what is produced, how it is produced, and how the products are exchanged. From this point of view, the final causes of all social changes and political revolutions are to be sought, not in men's brains, not in men's better insights into eternal truth and justice, but in changes in the modes of production and exchange. They are to be sought, not in the philosophy, but in the economics of each particular epoch. [35]

33   John Lame Deer,1973, *Lame Dear – Seeker of Visions*, Touchstone
34   Engels 1880 *Socialism – Utopian and Scientific* available at https://www.marxists.org/archive/marx/works/1880/soc-utop/ch03.htm accessed on 1.2.21
35   ibid

In this last quote, Engels identifies that classes in society are identified by their position relative to how production is organised and wealth created, ie the relations of production[36].

The 'Materialist Conception of History' is a theory that not only explains the roles that classes perform within each individual society but also how distinct societies develop and transform. It is not a fixed view and does not suggest everything is pre-determined. All that is being said is that the material conditions at any given time in any given society have an impact on what happens and on what people do and say. These conditions provide a framework for the possibilities for human activity. It enables us therefore to see the relationship between the physical world and the ideas as they progress through society and the relationship between ideas and social change.

Furthermore this explains why differing behaviours and beliefs emerge in different societies because the ideas that dominate in any given society are the ideas of the ruling class and more specifically ideas that justify and perpetuate the existing system[37].

Marx's historical materialism is an analysis of social structure[38] and this helps us understand how different human societies form and develop, and ultimately how any given society reaches the limit of its development and gives way to a more dynamic society. Hence, it is not correct to see primitive communism, slave society, feudalism and currently capitalism as a single process leading to today's society but perhaps as a series of stepping stones that, yes, lead us to today, but are more like distinct islands on which humanity needs to gain experience and expand its energy reserves before it can take the next step forward.

At a certain stage of development, the material productive forces[39] **of society come into conflict with the existing relations of production or** – this merely expresses the same thing in legal terms – **with the property relations** within the framework of which they have operated hitherto. From forms of development of the productive forces these relations turn into their fetters. Then begins an era of social revolution. The changes in the economic foundation

---

36 The relations of production are the totality of relationships within the mode of production between actors in society involved in the production and distribution of goods. Of further relevance here is the idea of the means of production which are the physical factors required ie capital assets, raw materials and components, the available technology and the working class itself that are required to undertake production. The relations of production are how that means of production is acted upon by groups of people in society..

37 Marx, 1845, *German Ideology* : "The ideas of the ruling class are in every epoch the ruling ideas, i.e. the class which is the ruling material force of society, is at the same time its ruling intellectual force. The class which has the means of material production at its disposal, has control at the same time over the means of mental production, so that thereby, generally speaking, the ideas of those who lack the means of mental production are subject to it. The ruling ideas are nothing more than the ideal expression of the dominant material relationships, the dominant material relationships grasped as ideas."

38 This is what marxists mean when they say marxism is a science.

39 The means of production or the productive forces are the machinery and/or equipment used, the raw materials, the working population and the technology that exists

lead sooner or later to the transformation of the whole immense superstructure. [40] (*My emphasis*)

Each mode of production forms a unique society then, one which develops a combination of productive forces, new technologies and improved social systems to make use of those technologies. It grows until it reaches a limit set internally by the capacity of humanity to use that technology (we will return to this idea shortly). When a society reaches this limit, there comes a period of stagnation or decay. The old technologies are still being used but humanity starts looking for new ways to improve its capacity to support the population of society. Necessity is the mother of invention as they say, so what gradually emerges from that problematic situation is a new set of relations of production, a new mode of production, which has the capacity to develop technology and the means of production further. This new set of relations of production is introduced and developed by a new class, not necessarily consciously, for this new ruling class is following its own interests and developing its own position as a ruling class.

What is most significant for us today is that Luxemburg and others were able to recognise that the growing conflicts leading to WW1 represented the point in society's development where conflict was taking over and hence the start of a period when 'the material productive forces of society come into conflict with the existing relations of production' as per the previous quote from Marx. This analysis was a recognition that capitalism had reached the limit of its growth and its decline would set the scenario for the possibility of a step forward into socialism.

Before we discuss an analysis of the stage capitalism has reached in the Chapter 5, it is important to look at the evidence that Luxemburg (amongst others) presented on just how these previous societies differed from capitalism and in particular the impact of what we call economics.

Marx identified that the relations of production were the basis on which each society was organised so the following sections will explain in more detail the relations of production for slave, feudal and capitalist society (ie the 3 main types of class society that appeared in history). These sections will show how each of these societies produce value and how that value is distributed between the sections of each society that we called classes.

This brief overview of historical materialism demonstrates that human behaviour must be viewed in a historical context.

> Men make their own history, but they do not make it as they please; they do not make it under self-selected circumstances, but under circumstances existing already, given and transmitted from the past. The tradition of all dead generations weighs like a nightmare on the brains of the living. [41]

---

40   Marx, 1859, *Preface to A Contribution to the Critique of Political Economy*, *available at* *https://www.marxists.org/archive/marx/works/1859/critique-pol-economy/preface.htm* accessed on 1.2.21

41   Marx, 1852, *The 18th Brumaire of Louis Bonaparte* available at https://www.marxists.org/archive/marx/works/1852/18th-brumaire/ch01.htm accessed

An Overview of the
History of Class Society

With this overview of how to look at history, let us now look at the slave society, feudalism and capitalism and focus on why they were different, how they were organised and how wealth was created.

Slave Society

In slave society, production was based on what physical human power and simple tools could achieve.

The organisation of society in Ancient Greece is presented by bourgeois historians as the foundation of so-called democracy but what they conveniently forget is that Greece was a slave society. Democratic type systems were reserved for the ruling class alone but the work on which they all depended was done by slaves. It wasn't a particularly wealthy society but the ruling class did lead a cushioned life which enabled them to begin investigations into sciences and philosophy and to indulge in pastimes like sports and writing. They were only able to do this though because almost 50% of the population were slaves.

Whilst the ruling class had given themselves the free time and opportunity to develop rudimentary sciences, their ideas were also limited by the world they saw about them. They indulged themselves in sports and wars. They saw gods everywhere and worshipped them because they couldn't explain everything that happened in the world. Technical progress was focussed particularly on building technologies in order to produce mausoleums for the dead and temples for the gods.

The Romans also developed important road building skills that were essential to its capacity to expand and maintain contact within the empire. They had no conception however of things such as the equality[42], nations and nationalism, finance or economics. Famous for its emperors and the decadent lifestyle provided for the ruling class as well as the size of the empire that it built, the Roman empire nevertheless relied on bringing in more slaves to increase the luxurious lifestyle of the upper classes and to provide their entertainment.

When the Roman Empire met the limits of its expansion, it had become an enormous empire that had spread across N Africa, Middle East and most of Europe. It had basically become too large and too costly to maintain and the empire began to find itself under threat from the barbarian tribes simply because it was just stretched too far to defend itself. Also conflicts within the Roman ruling class began to weaken the control over the Empire. When the Empire weakened and broke down, smaller family groupings and warlords began to establish control

---

42   Slavery was the norm but racism appears not to have been a feature of their society.

over smaller areas of land and these holdings eventually, over a period of centuries, became the royalty and nobility of the feudal system.

This type of economic structure may have provided a luxurious lifestyle for the ruling class but it was a fairly static form of society that only developed very slowly. The Greek ruling class found time to think and write and philosophise, to investigate basic sciences such as mathematics and the study of the stars and even developed some hydraulic technologies and a famous mechanical computer[43] but did not have the economic structures in place to develop these ideas further. The Romans expanded technology enough to develop basic engineering skills and were able to produce hydraulic and steam appliances[44].

However, slave societies were limited in their capacity to apply technologies to everyday life and, fundamentally, if something needing doing then you just go out and get more slaves to do all the work manually. This is a perfect example of Marx's theory, where the relations of production – slaves owned by slaveholders – limits the expansion of the production forces.

It is true that these societies used money to some extent but they were not a market economies with shops selling all the day to day needs for the population. The exchange of goods whether using money or not, was primarily to supplement what each household could produce and to dispose of surpluses. It was a planned economy comprised of households in which slaves were organised by their owners to produced the means of subsistence for the whole household. The status of slaves, slaveowners and other layers of society were fixed in law. Probably the major use of money and indeed taxation at that time was to pay for the emperor and for the armed forces. Trade was primarily in luxuries for the benefit of the ruling classes.

How was value created in slave society then?

Each household owned slaves to do the work of the providing the means of subsistence for the entire household. The household owned the slaves body and soul, it owned all the equipment these workers used and all the products of their labour. The work done was planned and controlled by the household. The slaves nevertheless had to be provided with a roof over their heads and their means of subsistence – this obviously came out of their own labour but the household took all the surplus produced. Wealth was judged not by an accumulation of money or even the values of possessions because in this system, with these very simple but brutal relations of production, it just wasn't necessary to use money for production purposes. Wealth was judged by the amount of land and buildings and slaves that the household owned and by the contents of those buildings. The longer the list of possessions, the better the status of the household. The more glamorous the contents of these buildings, the more glamorous the clothing and

---

43 The Antikythera Mechanism was a small, hand operated computer for mapping the stars – it was lost at sea until the 20th Century and the technology itself was lost to humanity until the 15th century

44 "All right... all right... but apart from better sanitation and medicine and education and irrigation and public health and roads and a freshwater system and baths and public order... what *have* the Romans done for *us*?" from Monty Python's Life of Brian

the food available to the household, the wealthier it would have been perceived by the rest of society.

It is worth noting that the word economy is derived from its use in the greek language at this time. "Oikos" means house or household and "nomos" means management. It related therefore to the household as the basic building block of slave society and its management of resources and not, as you can see, to the handling of money or the recording of values. This transferred into Latin where the word "*oeconomicus*" meant domestic economy.

As explained by Luxemburg:

> Let us turn to a Greek *oikos*, the household economy of antiquity with slaves, which by and large also formed a "microcosm," a little world unto itself. Here extreme social inequality already prevails. Primitive need has been transformed into a comfortable surplus of the fruits of human labor. Physical labor has become the curse of some, idleness the privilege of others, with those who work even becoming the property of the non-workers. Yet here again, this relationship of domination involves the strictest planning and organization of the economy, the labor process and distribution. The determining will of the master is its foundation, the whip of the slave overseer its sanction.[45]

Feudalism

In feudal society, human power still ruled but society was based on land and agriculture. Technical progress in agriculture and clothing but also in household products, ships and weaponry enabled a greater rate of growth in society as a whole. In the realm of ideas, loyalty and obedience to the masters in society was not quite unquestioned but was certainly expected and was indeed part of what made this society more efficient that slave society. Chivalry was in fact the set of rules by which wars and battles were fought. Nationalities did not exist as the kingdoms were bounded by the borders established in last conflict. The workers, ie serfs, were not owned by the ruling class but their social status was still legally defined and virtually invariable. There was still no conception of the equality of human beings, nationality or nationalism and economics. Feudal relations of production installed very fixed and legalised structures of property and status in society but these still limited development.

It took several centuries for feudal society to fully form itself after the collapse of the Roman Empire and what emerged was a system of kings and queens who owned and disposed of all of the territory they controlled as well as its contents. Despite this, the state was relatively decentralised. Royalty retained ultimate control and ownership of the land and all possessions within but they granted fiefdoms to the nobility who in their turn granted rights to the Lords of the Manor and, in turn, serfs were granted rights to work parcels of land for their own

---

45   Luxemburg, What is Economics in Mary Alice Walters 1970 *Rosa Luxemburg Speaks* Pathfinder Press

upkeep. The serfs had to provide tithes (ie the form of food and products) in return however. The lords and nobility also provided service and loyalty to their kings. It was essentially a system based on the provision of land and authority in return for labour or service with the status of all individuals established in law.

Figure 3 The Structure of Feudalism [46]

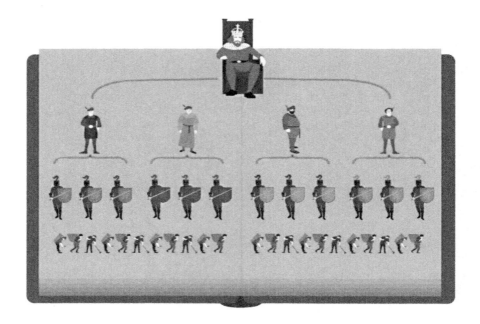

Luxemburg used the example of Charlemagne[47], the feudal king who in the 9th Century ruled over most of what is now France, Italy, Switzerland N Spain Holland and Belgium (he also became emperor of the Holy Roman Empire ie the area dominated by the catholic church but this was 4 centuries after the Roman Empire itself disintegrated):

> ...he wrote a special decree comprising seventy paragraphs in which he laid down the principles which were to be applied to the management of his farms: the famous Capitulare de Villis, I.e., law about the manors; fortunately this document, a priceless treasury of historical information, has been preserved to this day, among the moulder and dust of the archives. This document deserves particular attention, for two reasons. First of all, most of the agricultural holdings of Charlemagne subsequently developed into

---

46   BBC Bitesize, *Feudalism and the Domesday Book* available at
     https://www.bbc.co.uk/bitesize/guides/zdvdmp3/revision/5 accessed on 8.9.20
47   For a brief biography see BBC Bitesize
     http://www.bbc.co.uk/history/historic_figures/charlemagne.shtml)

mighty free cities. ... Secondly, the economic regulations of Charlemagne constituted a model for all the larger ecclesiastical and secular estates of the early Middle Ages; Charlemagne's manors kept the traditions of old Rome alive and transplanted the refined culture of the Roman villas into the rough milieu of the young Teutonic nobility; his regulations about winemaking, gardening, fruit and vegetable raising, poultry breeding, and so forth, were a historic achievement of lasting significance. [48]

So this emperor of mainland Europe laid down detailed rules for his nobility to follow in managing the lands he had allocated to them but what is so descriptive of the structure of feudal society is that he required his lords etc to undertake the same tasks within their lands:

Luxemburg provided excerpts from the 62nd paragraph of the document:

It is important that we know what and how much of each we own-of every article." And once more he lists them: oxen, mills, wood, boats, vines, vegetables, wool, linen, hemp, fruits, bees, fishes, hides, wax, and honey, new and aged wines, and other things which are delivered to him. And for the consolation of his dear vassals who are to supply him with all these things, he adds guilelessly: We hope that all this shall not appear too difficult for you; since each of you is lord on his manor, you, La turn, may exact these things from your subjects. [49]

We can also use the example of the Domesday Book in England. When William became King of England by invading England and defeating the previous monarch Harold, he took possession of the people and lands within it and distributed fiefdoms to the loyal nobility from Normandy who had taken part in the invasion. He was now King of England and Normandy but he knew little of what he owned so the Domesday Book was commissioned to detail all his possessions in England. Again no value, no measure of accumulated wealth to be held in bank accounts, simple a list of physical possessions.

On the feudal manor of the Middle Ages, this despotic organization of labor has the manifestation of a detailed code elaborated in advance, **in which the plan and division of labor, the duties of each as well as their claims, are clearly and firmly defined**. On the threshold of this period of history stands that fine document that we have already cited: Charlemagne's "*Capitulare de villis*," which still revels joyously and brightly in the wealth of physical enjoyments to which the economy is completely directed. At its end we have the baneful code of services and dues which, dictated by the unrestrained financial greed of the feudal lords, led to the German peasant war of the sixteenth century, and made the French peasant still 200 years later into that miserable and semi-bestialized

---

48 Luxemburg, What is Economics in Mary Alice Walters 1970 *Rosa Luxemburg Speaks* Pathfinder Press
49 ibid

25

creature who was only shaken to struggle for his human and civil rights by the shrill alarm clock of the great Revolution. But, until the broom of revolution swept away the feudal manor, this peasant was still in the misery of the relationship of direct mastery that firmly and clearly defined the relations of the feudal economy as an unavoidable fate. [50] (my emphasis)

Ultimately therefore Luxemburg was able to identify significant common ground between how the sovereigns of this time set objectives and techniques for managing their households and these rules were also applied to both the nobility and the serfs under them. Please note that none of this required financial accounting or the recording of values. They only needed to know the content of their households physically and whether it was sufficient for their needs.

The small farmer on his plot of land as well as the great sovereign on his manors, - both of them know exactly what they to accomplish in production. And what is more, neither has to be a genius to know it. Both want to satisfy the ordinary hum requirements of food, drink cloths, and to obtain the various comforts of life. The only difference is that the peasant sleeps on a straw mat, while the noble lord sleeps in a soft feather bed. ... [51]

These roles were fixed in law and whoever broke with these rules became 'outlaws' living out in the forests. Fans of the Robin Hood stories may think this sounds familiar but this situation was also part of the origins of capitalism within feudalism as the Birmingham and Black Country areas in the UK became a draw for discontented craftspeople etc. It was an area where the raw materials were particularly suitable for the establishment of new industrial enterprises and the development of new technologies that would come to highlight the weakness of feudal production and contribute greatly to the industrial revolution

Just as with the slave households of previous times, there was no economy outside of the list of possessions owned by each feudal household. Everything that the serfs and their families needed were self produced and the local lords and nobility received a share of produce from all the serfs under their control. The households of the lords and nobility therefore had to include all the products they needed for their subsistence. Consequently it was necessary to ensure their serfs and craftspeople were producing the correct goods. This was still a planned economy although surpluses would have been exchanged and bartered. The maintenance of the court and the kIng's armies and knights were still the major use of money.

The question of how value was created in feudal society must now be explained.

The roles of the various classes in society were fixed in law. The ruling class owned the land and all its contents but the serfs, the feudal working class, were not slaves. They had a legal status and protections unlike the slaves of previous years and they had legal rights to use the respective parcels of land allocated to

---

50 ibid
51 ibid

26

them to produce their own subsistence. However, the serf only owned part of the produce of their labour as they were required to provide a percentage of their produce to the lord of the manor and a similar percentage to the church[52]. These tithes were taken by the local lord in payment for granting the use of the land. This particular set of relations of production meant that the serf retained the subsistence part of his labour but the surplus labour and surplus produce was effectively owned by the feudal nobility[53]. In some areas, feudal society required 'corvée' which meant serfs had to do a day's work unpaid for the lord of the manor.

Serfs also owed duty to the local lords and nobility and were frequently required to join the army to support either the lord or the king in their endeavours to defend or expand the lands they dominated.

In terms of social development, feudalism facilitated particularly the growth of agriculture including the use windmills and watermills to process food, also armaments technologies from gunpowder to castles as well as cultural developments related to religion (ie beliefs based on a single god) and the arts. Indeed cultural and scientific development was controlled by the church during this time. In the towns, guilds were used to organise and control craftworkers.

As surplus wealth grew in society, it was turned particularly towards foreign trade as the merchants began to bring in new products for the ruling class from overseas. By this means, the merchant class became wealthier and more important in society. As this wealth grew further, it began to be invested not just in trade but in manufacture where it was discovered that even greater profits could be earned. Gradually these new relations of production began to dominate in society as they provided a more efficient system to make use of the new technologies that were emerging. Eventually the bourgeoisie, the town dwellers who could earn vast sums and outstrip the power and influence of the nobility, emerged to take over and dominate society.

Just as the feudal system of agriculture developed within a declining slavery-based society, the bourgeoisie in the form of merchants and financiers[54] grew in power and influence within feudal society. Both were revolutionary classes in these early years of growth and brought with them new relations of production and had to confront the old ruling class to be able to use them fully.

This was not necessarily a smooth process. The Roman empire disintegrated leading to a period known as the dark ages (from the 5th century onwards) and even when the feudal structures came to emerge (from the 9th century), humanity had in many ways taken a step backwards in terms of development.

The bourgeoisie did not bring an instant transformation and the conflict between the conservative feudal powers and the revolutionary bourgeoisie took place over an extended period from the 15th to the 19th Century before capitalism was able

---

52   In feudal England these tithes were 10% in each case.

53   Note that this surplus produce is not a commodity for sale and exchange on a market.

54   The first UK joint stock companies, a forerunner of today's limited companies, were founded during the 16th century during the reign of Elizabeth I to support piratical and colonial ventures.

to become fully dominant. In Europe there were continual local conflicts between feudal nobility and the emerging merchant classes[55] and open civil war often erupted to bring about the downfall of feudal empires even if those taking part didn't always realise what was going on eg the French revolution, the English civil war, American war of independence and also the American civil war. The confrontation between Catholic and Protestant churches during the reformation and afterwards was a 'symbolic' battle between feudal and bourgeois powers respectively.

Capitalism

In capitalist society, 'economics' has come into its own, although it was first known as 'political economy' (and sometimes national economy) by the theoreticians to differentiate it from the household economy.

Under capitalism, workers no longer produce for themselves or their own subsistence so it does not matter to workers what they produce. They create commodities which are sold on a competitive market. In this system, the capitalist owns not only everything that is needed for production but also the products of that production. This means that the owners of the means of production also have direct control of the product and the wages paid and hence are able to invest and produce better and better systems for making profits for themselves - in fact they absolutely have to do this continually to compete with the other owners. Workers therefore have no control over what is produced and who it is for whereas the capitalist class is free to create factories, build larger scale production, keep increasing productivity and sell its products in the marketplace. So whilst an individual business or factory in which workers are employed may be well structured and organised (labour is socialised labour as Marx and Engels called it), once the products leave the factory they are sold on a global market which has little or no structure or organisation. In this system, wealth grows in the hand of the capitalist, but workers continue to live just on subsistence wages. As we saw earlier, Luxemburg highlighted this marketplace as the domination of anarchy over society because the capitalists, politicians or economics professors cannot control what happens in the economy.

The separation of the workers from the product of their labour and the private ownership by capitalists of manufacturing equipment and the product of that labour is what enables mass production and the ongoing creation of wealth in the hands of the capitalist, yet restricts all individual workers to earnings that are only enough to live on.

Production is of commodities for sale in markets, commodities over which the workers hold no ownership, so whatever they actually produce, workers must buy all their subsistence goods from markets and shops. In this system, money needs to be used to conduct all the buying and welling and work must be paid labour. For this system to function, workers must legally be free individuals able to move and be moved, but they must also be absolutely dependent on the need to work to earn their means of subsistence (hence the term wage slaves). This apparent

---

55   Luxemburg, The Middle Ages, Feudalism Development of the Cities in Hudis (ed) 2013
     The Complete Works of Rosa Luxemburg Volume 1,   Verso

freedom from serfdom brought many painful experiences as they were forced off the land to work and live in dreadful conditions in the towns. However this change enabled the means of production to expand significantly and made capitalism the most dynamic form of class society.

> Feudalism overcame slavery because it allowed men to subsist without depending on the pillage of other populations; in its turn, capitalism imposed itself historically in the face of feudalism's collapse, through its ability to allow the concentration of human and material productive forces that the fragmentation of society into autonomous and jealously isolated fiefdoms made impossible. [56]

Luxemburg vividly describes capitalism in 'What is Economics':

> Today we have neither masters nor slaves, neither feudal barons nor serfs. Freedom and equality before the law have in formal terms done away with all despotic relationships, at least in the old bourgeois states; in the colonies, as is well known, these same states have frequently themselves introduced slavery and serfdom. Everywhere that the bourgeoisie is at home, *free competition* rules economic relations as their one and only law. This means the disappearance from the economy of any kind of plan or organization. Of course, if we look at an individual private firm, a modern factory or a large complex of factories and plants such as Krupp's, alternatively a great agricultural enterprise such as those of North America, we find here the strictest organization, the most far-reaching division of labor, the most refined planning based on scientific knowledge. Here everything works beautifully, directed by a *single* will and consciousness. But we scarcely leave the factory or farm gate than we are met already with chaos. Whereas the countless individual components – and a private firm today, even the most gigantic, is only a fragment of the great economic network that extends across the whole earth – whereas the fragments are most. [57]

The emergence of capitalism and the ultimate completion of its dominance over society during the 19th Century meant the establishment of a highly dynamic society that rapidly grew in size and was able to develop its technological capacities in a way that slave and feudal society was totally incapable of. In fact, previous societies had grown so slowly that it was only when capitalism emerged and took control that social sciences capable of investigating the dynamics of social change were even necessary let alone possible.

> For nearly all of human history, economic advance has been so slow as to be imperceptible within the span of a lifetime. For century after century, the annual rate of economic growth was, to one place of decimals, zero. When growth did happen, it was so slow as to be

---

56 ICC, 1982, *Crisis Theory.* in International Review 29
57 Luxemburg, What is Economics in Mary Alice Walters 1970 *Rosa Luxemburg Speaks* Pathfinder Press

invisible to contemporaries—and even in retrospect it appears not as rising living standards (which is what growth means today), merely as a gentle rise in population. Down the millennia, progress, for all but a tiny elite, amounted to this: it slowly became possible for more people to live, at the meanest level of subsistence. From about 1750, this iron law of history was broken. Growth began to be no longer invisibly slow nor confined, as it largely had been before, to farming. The new increase in human productivity was staggeringly large.[58]

Capitalism is an unplanned economy where exchange has replaced the planned use of labour and production[59], this means that society lacks overall organisation. Workers have legal freedom but they depend on others for the work that will provide their means of subsistence and that means unemployment and poverty are a continuous threat.

Now we must ask how value is created under capitalism?

The means of production are put in place by the capitalist who also contracts workers to to be paid at a fixed price to do the work involved in created the final product.   Before the workers act however, the capitalists have in a collection of physical means of production in effect sitting around waiting to be transformed into a finished item.   Only the application of labour can bring about their transformation into finished goods and furthermore, because the workers' wages are fixed beforehand, this process creates finished goods that are worth far more than the individual components. When capitalists sell their products they make a profit over and above all costs incurred. The workers create the new value but they are never paid the full value of their labour. This is how profits are created for the owners[60]. As Marx explained, a portion of unpaid labour is contained within the products and this earns the capitalist what we call surplus value when these products are sold.

Capitalists employ workers to do the work and sell the produce at a profit – its as simple of that.

Businesspeople, politicians and economics theory will tell you that profit comes from the organisation of a firm by the capitalist, by the investment of the capitalist and by the process of buying and selling.   Marx proved this to be false and 'Wages, Price and Profit in the 21st Century'[61] explains why.

Wage labour, private property and commodity production form the basis of capitalist production and all the value it creates.

---

58   The Economist, *The Road to Riches* 23.12.99 accessed on 20.9.2
59   Luxemburg, The Middle Ages, Feudalism Development of the Cities in Hudis (ed) 2013 *The Complete Works of Rosa Luxemburg* Volume 1, Verso
60   Sutton P, 2020, *Wages Price and Profit in the 21st Century* available at https://www.amazon.co.uk/Wages-Price-Profit-21st-Century-ebook/dp/B089FJCPYF/ref=sr_1_4dchild=1&keywords=wages+price+and+profit&qid=1599516563&sr=8-4
61   ibid

Historical materialism demonstrates that human behaviour must always be viewed in a historical context. It is not enough to say that wars and money and exchange and the rulers and the ruled have always existed, that people have always been greedy or selfish because these things will have different meanings and purposes in different periods of history. You can learn nothing about people let alone society from such a point of view. Each society with its own relations of production generates a different set of codes of behaviour and ideas that are based upon these relations. So we don't ask why the primitive tribes didn't believe in a single god, why the Roman Empire didn't have border controls or why they didn't think of producing televisions to save everybody travelling to the amphitheatres or why the Magna Carta didn't suggest a voting system for elections or indeed why capitalism does not have members of a nobility that runs the local state. Its just not possible for these things to occur out of the right historical context'

To paraphrase Marx[62] again, we cannot chose the world we are born into. This world exists before we do and the conditions we find in it when we are born, determine the framework for our life, our ideas and our behaviour. The future however is built by us and our ingenuity in the world we find ourselves in.

---

62 Marx, 1952, *The Eighteenth Brumaire of Louis Bonaparte:* "Men make their own history, but they do not make it as they please; they do not make it under self-selected circumstances, but under circumstances existing already, given and transmitted from the past. The tradition of all dead generations weighs like a nightmare on the brains of the living."

Luxemburg and the
Ascendancy of Capitalism

We must now look at the progress of capitalism, the society we live in, and explain its achievements in a historical context.

It was clear to Luxemburg that Capitalism had been slowly been developing and gaining power in the midst of the feudal economy since the 15th Century:

> The tremendous discoveries, conquests, plundering forays into the newly discovered countries, the sudden large influx of precious metals from the new continent, the extensive spice trade with India, the voluminous slave trade which supplied African Negroes to American plantations: all of these factors created new riches and new desires in Western Europe, in a very short period of time. The small workshop of the guild artisan, with its thousand-and-one restrictions became a brake on the necessary Increase of production on its rapid progress. The big merchants overcame this obstacle by assembling the craftsmen in large manufactures beyond the jurisdiction of the cities, under the supervision of the merchants, relieved of the restrictive regulations of the guilds, the mechanics produced quicker and better. [63]

Luxemburg was writing in the last years of the 19th and the early years of the 20th centuries. She was able to identify the roles the nation state, nationalism, and the national economy were playing within the growth of capitalism. She clearly recognised the creation of these structures as the actions of a progressive capitalism that was facilitating its expansion and increasing its dominance over society. This dominance was bringing together the whole of the planet within one economic and social network, the world market.

The economics professors recognise that economics as a subject of study came into being late in the 18th Century but these professors do not want to link this to the emergence of capitalism because that would mean accepting what Luxemburg says, ie that economics is the study of capitalism and how to maintain its class rule.

They try to link the new subject of economics with the new areas of scientific study that emerged during the same period but we can clearly see that it is not a science but a belief, a preference or, in many cases, just wishful thinking. These professors just have not been able to come up with theories that maintain themselves in the face of the challenges that events in the sphere of national and world economy have thrown at them. They are running in arrears desperately trying to catch up and inevitably failing.

---

63 Luxemburg, What is Economics in Mary Alice Walters 1970 *Rosa Luxemburg Speaks* Pathfinder Press

What were the main developments of capitalism in its progressive period?

The break up of the feudal structures and the creation of the nation state and the national economy along with the rules and regulations that enabled the industrial revolution to flourish were key during this period up to the end of the 19th century. As we have seen capitalism is not like feudalism where the roles of workers and ruling class are defined in law from the very start. It is a society that needed to present everyone with individual political and economic freedom in order to be more dynamic than previous systems. It is a society that needs to maintain this pretence of freedom and normality in order to keep workers working for others and allow business owners and managers to exploit and make ever larger profits.

If workers are persuaded in the belief that it is all normal and that they are under control and cannot do anything to change the system, then the system continues. This is a material result of the power of the ruling ideology under capitalism

The creation of commodity production and exchange gave capitalists the commercial resources to expand production and develop new technologies rapidly, and this enabled the industrial revolution. Only 200 years ago, all we had were castles and wooden huts, tracks for roads, horse and cart transport, only sailors in sailing ships had any idea of what the rest of the world looked like. There were no supplies of water, gas and electricity let alone sewerage systems and rubbish collections. Now we have a global networks of trade and transport, instant news and communications systems from all parts of the world, complex city based systems of services and distribution supplying all personal needs and wants, road and public transport networks, social support and leisure structures and too much more to list.

Capitalism brought with it gains but it clearly hasn't eliminated wars and famines and poverty and prejudice - and it hasn't brought a society that truly cares for and incorporates all humanity equally. It is a society in which everything depends on money.

During the feudal period, the city was the basis for the growth of commercial merchants but once capitalism was in control it needed a far greater economic area. Capitalism brought about the creation of the nation as a framework for the types of commercial and industrial rules and regulations that could enhance this growth.

The nation state therefore emerged to manage society but remained a small institution during the period when private capitalism dominated. However, it was able to establish the national borders and put in place the technical standards and the trading rules and regulations that would enable commerce to flourish within its boundaries. What emerged at this time were national systems of standardised measurements, times, coinage, payments and banking systems and transport systems. This process also needed nationalism to get everyone motivated to work and fight for the homeland and succumb to the various ideologies of superiority over other nationalities. The nation state remained a relatively small institution up until the late 1800s. Private industry dominated and set its own rules within the factories and in the market and little in the way of social security measures existed at this time, even the police force was new and limited in scope.

By the end of the 19th century it became accepted that the state would establish a bureaucracy to manage the legal rule and regulations it applied both for industry and the population in general. The state by this time had also taken the management of the armed forces out of private hands and established itself as the prime focus for relationships with other nations.

The rush to colonise at the end of the 19th century followed a long period when capital had sought to expand into further areas of the globe through private charter companies[64] who searched out resources, valuable minerals and foodstuffs and cheap labour to enrich themselves and their home countries. The end of the 19th century was the start of the period of imperialism as the states grabbed the final remaining undeveloped areas of the world as colonies. National economies in the major nations were fully established and grown to virtually complete their national boundaries. Economic growth and trade, with colonial expansion pretty much completed, now required and developed into intense international competition and this again changed the structures required in each nation.

By the start of the 20th Century, capital had expanded and effectively created what we now see as a global economy. Complex social systems were built not just within towns and nations but now a world market meant all nations were linked and dependent on one another. This inter-dependence of all nations has been continually reinforced since that time.

There is no specific date to fixate on, but WW1 has become a useful marker with which to describe the end to this period of ascendancy as Luxemburg clearly recognised. It marked the completion of national economies and their integration into a capitalism's world market. The period of a progressive capitalism was at an end.

We should not see the ascendant period of capitalism purely as a period of great gains for the world however. It also brought many negative factors that have been a real cost for humanity. It was a period of brutal transformation that generated slums worldwide as peasants were thrown of the land and had to move into the towns to search for work. This created poverty, illness and deprivation for workers who couldn't grow their own subsistence anymore, as well as creating a dependence of the working class on those with wealth and it did this by destroying the reliability and self-sufficiency of life on the land. Throughout the world indigenous peoples were murdered and brutalised by the transformation of their natural economies into capitalist society and the wars in the 20th century have brought death and destruction on a scale never seen before. Capitalism also brought with it the exploitation on a mass scale of the worlds' resources which began the depletion of stocks of fish and larger sea-life, wild animals, trees as well as mineral resources. Perhaps capitalists in those early days did not realise the impact of their activities on the environment but they certainly do now and they still cannot control those impulses.

---

64 Dalrymple, 2020, *The Anarchy: The Relentless Rise of the East India Company* Bloomsbury

Decadence and Obsolescence

The completion of the world market and the entry into WW1 brought in a new phase which corresponds to the period in which: '... the material productive forces of society come into conflict with the existing relations of production' [65]. This is a significant milestone because it changes the possibilities for capitalism's development ie it changes how the internal contradictions affect one another[66].

These changes were preceded, as we know, by one final push by the established powers in a rampant rush to annex the remaining parts of the world to their own empires. Imperialism as it was called at the time was seen as a significant stage in the life of capitalism and a herald of every greater competition between powerful nations. Whilst the colonies gradually achieved legal independence from those empires during the 20th Century, they have for the most part never been able to achieve real independence nor a position of strength in the world. Imperialism has simply developed from a competition for colonies to a commercial, financial and political competition between all nations of the world, a competition that is inevitably dominated by the more powerful economic and military nations. It is a competition that leads inevitably to open warfare.

This intensification of competition between states escalates from the early 20th century and continues to provoke wars between nations and blocs of nations and becomes a major problem for humanity as a whole. Just like an ingrowing toenail, its growth continues but this growth has been perverted and it goes in the wrong direction, thereby causes major problems of instability and pain for the body as whole. For capitalism and its economists however, there are no nails to trim or toes to cut off! Competition certainly drives growth but it eventually leads to conflict and self-destructive actions. The consequence is continual disruption to the capacity of human society to grow in a healthy and constructive fashion.

Marx was particularly dramatic in his explanation of the end result of capitalism:

> The bourgeois period of history has to create the material basis of the new world — on the one hand universal intercourse founded upon the mutual dependency of mankind, and the means of that intercourse; on the other hand the development of the productive powers of man and the transformation of material production into a scientific domination of natural agencies. Bourgeois industry and commerce create these material conditions of a new world in the same way as geological revolutions have created the surface of the earth. When a great social revolution shall have mastered the results of the bourgeois epoch, the market of the world and the modern powers of production, and subjected them to the common

---

65 Marx, 1858, *The First Indian War of Independence 1857-1858*
    https://www.marxists.org/archive/marx/works/1857/india/index.tm accessed on 1.2.21
66 Engels, 1880, *Social Utopian and Scientific*
    https://www.marxists.org/archive/marx/works/1880/soc-utop/index.htm accessed on
    1.2.21

control of the most advanced peoples, then only will human progress cease to resemble that hideous, pagan idol, who would not drink the nectar but from the skulls of the slain. [67]

As a result of the change in conditions, since that time we have seen, just as Engels forecasted[68], the state apparatus taking on an ever greater role to manage society. This is precisely because competition between individual capitalists means they no longer manage society with the needs of the whole of the economy or society in mind. They look after themselves individually not capitalism as a whole.

To overcome the crises in the 19th Century, the markets were able to take a step back and allow for the periodic crises in production and circulation to gradually work themselves out[69] whereas, in this new period, government intervention and the use of credit in particular have become dominant factors in the management of crises. In recent years we can see that the response to the financial crisis of 2008 involved international cooperation between nation states to manage what some saw at the time as such a massive increase in debt that it would be just too great to overcome. Additionally, the response of the nation states worldwide during the coronavirus pandemic illustrates this difference because the financial arrangements and health systems put in place would have been impossible in the 19th century when the state was so small and lacking in influence and control. In the 21st century on the other hand, it is unimaginable that nation states would not respond to such crisis in some way to try to maintain economic stability – just as it is equally unimaginable that this money-based system would put health before money. That is clearly evident from the events of 2020.

A further result of the expanded role of the state is that ideological controls over society have become more significant. The 1st World War was widely understood to be an issue of international economics and there was little spin (as it is now called) put on the conflict to suggest it was anything other than that. It ended however with a wave of struggles by workers that directly threatened the control of the ruling class and since then all nation states has worked hard to put an ideological cover over all its conflicts. Such smokescreens have included nationalism, the defence of human rights, anti fascism, the defence of democracy or defence against aggressors. World War 2 became about freedom and anti fascism, the USSR and China became so-called communist states despite the brutality to their populations, state capitalism has become socialism and any right winger has become a fascist, and particularly importantly, nationalism is good.

67 Marx, 1858, _The First Indian War of Independence 1857-185_8 accessed on 1.2.21
68 Engels,1880, _Socialism Utopian and Scientific_: "... the modern State, again, is only the organization that bourgeois society takes on in order to support the external conditions of the capitalist mode of production against the encroachments as well of the workers as of individual capitalists. The modern state, no matter what its form, is essentially a capitalist machine — the state of the capitalists, the ideal personification of the total national capital. The more it proceeds to the taking over of productive forces, the more does it actually become the national capitalist, the more citizens does it exploit. The workers remain wage-workers — proletarians. The capitalist relation is not done away with. It is, rather, brought to a head"
69 See Engels, 1880, _Social Utopian and Scientific_
    https://www.marxists.org/archive/marx/works/1880/soc-utop/index.htm accessed on 1.2.21

These ideological mystifications are important to keeping workers passive and keep them working.

It is noticeable that global GDP has continued to grow as has the world population but this only means that while the wealthy have got wealthier, the ever larger numbers of poor remain poor. This growth during the last century has only been possible because of the increased used of credit systems so large that only the centralised state apparatus can manage them. According to the Institute of International Finance, world debt now equals over three times the level of world GDP and worse, household debt is now well over 50% of world GDP[70]. This is not the situation a healthy society would find itself in! Capitalism clearly is not working well as a financial and commercial system.

The changes in conditions at the start of the 20th century initiated a period which can be described variously as decay, degeneration, decomposition and obsolescence [71]. That might sound dramatic but just think of what we have seen since that time:

- 2 World Wars,
- a 40 year cold war between the USA and the USSR
- the stockpiling of nuclear arsenals
- incessant regional wars
- the growth of centralised state capitalism and its control over social, political and economic fields
- the growth of debt and credit systems not just for the state but for individuals and households too
- ever more intense exploitation of workers
- ever greater ideological control over the population by the state
- migration crises
- famines
- global warming
- rising ocean levels
- rising ocean temperatures
- floods and fires
- destruction of wildlife
- health pandemics as products of the intensity of city life and animal trade
- the potential for environmental and/or military catastrophe

The list just goes on and on, doesn't it! [72]

Whilst it is true to suggest that not everything we see during this period of decay is negative, this however is not the point when considering if the system is in decline. The world economy continues to grow at a pace much greater than at

---

70   IIF 6.7.2020 *Global Debt Monitor* available at https://www.iif.com/Portals/0/Files/content/Research/Global%20Debt%20Monitor_July2020.pdf? Accessed on 14.10.20
71   See Matthew White, *The Great Big Book of Horrible Things – The Definitive Chronicle of History's Worst 100 Atrocities.* Norton & Co, Atrocitology and Necrometrics appear to be special new sciences for capitalist decadence which is about the measurement or estimation of the death toll and the figures are awful
72   Roberts M, 2020, *Covid and the Challenges for Capitalism* Youtube interview.

any time in history (ie both in absolute and percentage terms) and technological development has been particularly marked with significant advances in medical, materials and manufacturing technologies and particularly in the later part of the 20th Century with the move into computerisation, artificial intelligence and bio-genetics. However after consideration of these gains, we are nevertheless left with the question of what might have been had these advances been used properly.   The level of destruction and waste that has accompanied this period, through competition and the lack of cooperation, through wars, and through waste industries like arms production (even if they are not actually used), insurance and financial industries, has been enormous. What we can say is that the means of production that now exist are sufficient to create a society of abundance for all but the relations of production, those systems that define what capitalism is, are just holding back society from any real step forward.

The coronavirus pandemic also demonstrates just how money itself stands in the way of a truly humane society precisely because of the conflicts between financial considerations and health concerns in managing the situation. It has necessitated a reversal of all those austerity policies of recent decades and has seen the enormous expansion of debts which will leave the system in who knows what sort of difficulties in future.

It also demonstrates just how inappropriate capital is in the modern world of high populations, mega-cities and easy transport.   Money considerations have totally prevented adequate responses by the nation states in terms of looking after the health of their populations and the environment. Private property locks away the skills and technologies needed to improve the lot of humanity as a whole because, in this era of advanced technology, it has all become just too expensive to share with people, whereas, as Richard Wolff points out in this video [73] about a declining capitalism, they can afford to stockpile vast amounts of weaponry. As suggested earlier, his descriptions are good but he still thinks that more state involvement can put capitalism right!

Does it irritate you when you see how wealthy the footballers, pop stars and movie stars have become in the past half century? Ok, they may have great skills but why do they deserve such riches when all those key workers that were newly discovered during the coronavirus pandemic live on basic wages? How does this absurdity come about? It is simply a byproduct of a dependence on markets - entertainers nowadays have an international market for their product today rather than just a local one!   Films, CDs and sports have gained billions of customers in the global economy and can therefore earn fortunes from sales to large audiences.

In July 2020, the CEO of Amazon, Jeff Bezos, found that he had become $10billion richer in just one day because of the rise in value of Amazon shares during the pandemic[74].   He is another example of how someone who runs a

73   Wolff R, 2020, *Is Capitalism on Life Support?* Available at
     https://www.youtube.com/watch?v=QZcYtJmGqa0 accessed on 1.2.21
74   Guardian Online. 2020, Jeff Bezos
     (https://www.theguardian.com/technology/2020/jul/21/jeff-bezos-the-worlds-richest-man-added-10bn-to-his-fortune-in-just-one-day). Accessed on 21.7.20

business that has a massive audience in the global market can become massively wealthy at the expense of the rest of us, for example:

> Between 1990 and 2020, U.S. billionaire wealth soared 1,130 percent in 2020 dollars, an increase more than 200 times greater than the 5.37 percent growth of U.S. median wealth over this same period ... Between 1980 and 2018, the tax obligations of America's billionaires, measured as a percentage of their wealth, decreased 79 percent. [75]

The shenanigans on the financial markets in 2008 brought the banking sector to the brink of collapse and led to the imposition of austerity on the rest of us whilst government propped up the already rich. The financial sector was able to offer the rich greater profits than from investment in production and the consequence has been that the corruptness of the financial system is highlighted and the obsolescence of money and financial system becomes ever more obvious.

> From 1948 to 1979 (*in the USA that is*), worker productivity grew by 108.1% and wages grew by 93.2% with the stock market growing by 603%. By contrast from 1979 to 2018, worker productivity grew by 69.6%, but the wealth created by these productivity gains went predominantly to executives and stockholders. Worker pay rose by only 11.6 % during this period, while compensation for chief executives grew by an enormous 940% and the stock market grew by 2200%.[76]

Let's be blunt. It is not enough to say that money is merely inappropriate today, it is absurd and obscene.   The Covid pandemic its clearly continuing for some time.   Governments have financially supported workers and businesses to some extent but it can't keep on paying endlessly, yet business keep screaming for more support to keep the going and more and more workers are ending up unemployed. While because of this pandemic, the billionaires are getting richer[77].

Drugs are locked away from the sick because the pharmaceutical companies cannot make enough profit; clean water is stolen from the water table in Africa to fill bottles when local people drink from dirty streams; peasant farmers in South America struggle to live collecting coca leaves so drugs barons in across the world can make fortunes; peasant farmers in Africa supply cash crops so that Europeans can eat cheaply yet their local society lacks foods for subsistence; animals are shipped from Europe to abattoirs in the Middle East because it is cheaper to slaughter them there; car engines are manufacturing in Mexico then

---

75   Institute of Policy Research 2020, Billionaire Bonanza 2020. https://ips-dc.org/wp-content/uploads/2020/04/Billionaire-Bonanza-2020.pdf?fbclid=IwAR0GfhUNc2s6ymkm2UKl6cYFldTb-MTrkL-AsLs1F8QDUKp7OpY5E7Yz-Zl Accessed on 20.9.20
76   Strine & Zwillinger, 2020, *What Milton Friedman missed about Social Inequality* The New York Times 10.9.2020
77   "... billionaires increased their wealth by more than a quarter (27.5%) at the height of the crisis from April to July, just as millions of people around the world lost their jobs or were struggling to get by on government schemes". Guardian 7.10.20 Billionaires' wealth rises to $10.2 trillion amid Covid crisis accessed on 14.10.20

shipped to car builders in Europe; plastics fill up our seas because recyclable materials are too expensive; billions are spent on weapons that are stored away just in case; and more and more supermarkets get built when what's needed are more foodbanks.

It is money and private property that causes these obscenities, the money-based economy has gone mad.

What is clear is that, whilst all previous societies have been products of the scarcity of resources relative to the population, the dynamism of capitalism's expansion of the means of production means it has now brought us to the point where we could have a society of abundance.

Capitalism now stands in the way of any advance for humanity. It has created vast wealth of resources and skills, the capacity to maintain growth, a world market and a global working class. These are all the factors needed to create an advanced society of abundance, a socialist society. In this sense capitalism has outlived its usefulness, it is obsolete.

What we really are seeing is a system that is under pressure from itself. The relations of production, wage labour, commodity production and private property, just pose too many contradictions and problems for the system to be able to keep functioning in a healthy fashion. As a result we see that competition intensifies economically, politically and in the end militarily, overall profits to be had from production decline percentage wise, debt increases, inequality increases, costs need to be reduced and exploitation needs to be increased - all these factors combine to misuse the technical gains that capitalism has been able to achieve and end up just creating problems that capitalism itself cannot solve.[78]

At a time when the productive capacity of the world is so great, a money based system just defrauds the working population and accumulates wealth into fewer and fewer hands. It wastes resources protecting itself and fails to satisfy the human needs of the population as a whole. The capitalist economic system just does not distribute scarce resource to those in need, it stockpiles them for the wealthy.

Whatever else you believe about the world today, the economics professors clearly have not solved the problems of understanding how to manage the economy.

---

78 This text has described features of capitalism's problems in this last century but does not attempt to tackle precisely why crises emerge. The 3 main crises theories are the falling rate of profit, overproduction and the lack of capacity for market expansion.

Socialism or Barbarism

Luxemburg wrote 'The Junius Pamphlet' in 1915 as part of her work to organise a revolutionary working class response to WW1. The extract below shows a lot of foresight and can be seen as a template for viewing the period after WW1 even if things have not turned out exactly as Luxemburg thought.

> Friedrich Engels once said: "Bourgeois society stands at the crossroads, either transition to socialism or regression into barbarism." What does "regression into barbarism" mean to our lofty European civilization? Until now, we have all probably read and repeated these words thoughtlessly, without suspecting their fearsome seriousness. A look around us at this moment shows what the regression of bourgeois society into barbarism means. This world war is a regression into barbarism. The triumph of imperialism leads to the annihilation of civilization. At first, this happens sporadically for the duration of a modern war, but then when the period of unlimited wars begins it progresses toward its inevitable consequences. Today, we face the choice exactly as Friedrich Engels foresaw it a generation ago: either the triumph of imperialism and the collapse of all civilization as in ancient Rome, depopulation, desolation, degeneration – a great cemetery. Or the victory of socialism, that means the conscious active struggle of the international proletariat against imperialism and its method of war. This is a dilemma of world history, an either/or; the scales are wavering before the decision of the class-conscious proletariat. The future of civilization and humanity depends on whether or not the proletariat resolves manfully to throw its revolutionary broadsword into the scales. In this war imperialism has won. Its bloody sword of genocide has brutally tilted the scale toward the abyss of misery. The only compensation for all the misery and all the shame would be if we learn from the war how the proletariat can seize mastery of its own destiny and escape the role of the lackey to the ruling classes.. [79]

'The Junius Pamphlet' accepted that capitalist had reached the point where it had achieved so much that a new society had become possible. When that 'ascendant' period was complete, questions arose around questions of 'degeneration' and 'obsolescence' and of how much longer capitalism could last.

Its institutions for growth, the national economies, had now by and large become completed and fully established mechanisms. The state had by then gradually started to take over the management of the national economy and its international

---

79   Luxemburg, 1915, *The Junius Pamphlet*. Please not that it was not Engels that said this "Bourgeois society stands at the crossroads....." it is more likely that Luxemburg based this phrasing from Karl Kautsky's text entitled The Erfurt Programme https://www.marxists.org/archive/kautsky/1892/erfurt/index.htm accessed on 1.2.21

relationships. The world market was also by and large completed, capitalism dominated the world either through the universal domination of the waged labour and private property or by the domination of markets over areas that were not completely transformed into capitalist production.

> If it is the task and object of political economy to explain the laws of the origin, development and spread of the capitalist mode of production, it is an unavoidable consequence that it must as a further consequence also discover the laws of the decline of capitalism, which just like previous economic forms is not of eternal duration, but is simply a transitional phase of history, a rung on the endless ladder of social development. The doctrine of the emergence of capitalism thus logically turns into the doctrine of the decline of capitalism, the science of the mode of production of capital into the scientific foundation of socialism, the theoretical means of the bourgeoisie's domination into a weapon of the revolutionary class struggle for the liberation of the proletariat.[80]

That all societies have periods of growth and periods of decline, perhaps, should not be a surprise as after all we can see the same process in action within capitalism with regard to products, industries and even empires. However what does the decline of capitalism mean?   Marx, Engels, Luxemburg and others concluded that this decline could only lead to 2 broad alternatives - socialism or barbarism.

What we must now discuss is just what these 2 options mean and indeed why only these 2, why not a new form of exploitation and production?

To see how new societies emerge from old, it is necessary to identify a new class which brings along with it new economic relations that can replace the old set belonging to the previous society. However what Marx identified even at an early stage was that no new class existed or was emerging within capitalism to bring with it a new form of exploitation. Only 2 main classes were brought about by capitalist relations of production, the bourgeoisie, the ruling exploiting class, and the working class, the exploited class.[81]

---

80 Luxemburg in Hudis, P (ed.) (2013) *The Complete Works of Rosa Luxemburg*, Volume I: Economic Writings I. London: Verso Books

81 From Castoriadis, 1949, Socialism or Barbarism in Curtis (Ed) 1988 *Cornelius Castoriadis Political and Social Writings*: "...capitalism has created the objective premises for the proletarian revolution on a world scale. It has accumulated wealth. It has developed the forces of production. It has rationalized and organized production up to the very limits permitted by its own regime of exploitation. It has created and developed the proletariat, whom it has taught how to handle both the means of production and weapons, while at the same time imbuing it with a hatred of misery and slavery. But capitalism has exhausted its historical role. It can go no further. It has created an international, rationalized, and planned economic structure, thus making it possible for the economy to be directed consciously and for social life to develop freely. But capitalism is incapable of achieving for itself this conscious management of the economy, for it is a system based on exploitation, oppression, and the alienation of the vast majority of humankind."

History has clearly confirmed this analysis. There are no new classes and no new mode of production emerging within capitalism. The structures of capitalism's ruling class may have changed in certain respects and various theories have grown to try to justify state control and the state bureaucracy as a new from of class society, but in fact this change was also foreseen by Engels and others[82]. State capitalism is just a development of capitalist exploitation which protects and extends the life of the capitalist mode of production.

With no new class emerging, only the working class exists as a class which can create a new society, but the working class has no material benefits to protect within a society that only offers it subsistence income. This means that it has the capacity to see what society actually is, it needs no ideology to protect its property rights and therefore it does not bring a new form of exploitation either. Consequently, a working class revolution must be a conscious revolution; it happens because the working class become aware of its fight with the ruling class and when it takes power it does so to create a society in its own image, a society of equal workers.

If the working class does not successfully achieve a socialist revolution what else is possible? Well, if you can accept Marx's theory that societies grow but then decline because of internal limitations then you can understand how capitalism cannot just go on forever. Capitalism just cannot get rid of its internal contradictions. The economists keep failing to solve the economic problems and indeed simply recycle old ideas that lead nowhere, and the politicians are becoming more and more divided amongst themselves when it comes to how to run society. Luxemburg identified early in the 19th century that what was coming was a period of wars and revolutions. Lenin identified this new period as a period of imperialism, the last phase of capitalism and that this would lead to wars and revolutions. The 2 revolutionaries had different analyses but with a common theme developing Marx's idea of capitalism leading to the mutual ruin of all classes.

82　From Engels 1880 Socialism Utopian and Scientific, Part 3: "But, the transformation — either into joint-stock companies and trusts, or into State-ownership — does not do away with the capitalistic nature of the productive forces. In the joint-stock companies and trusts, this is obvious. And the modern State, again, is only the organization that bourgeois society takes on in order to support the external conditions of the capitalist mode of production against the encroachments as well of the workers as of individual capitalists. The modern state, no matter what its form, is essentially a capitalist machine — the state of the capitalists, the ideal personification of the total national capital. The more it proceeds to the taking over of productive forces, the more does it actually become the national capitalist, the more citizens does it exploit. The workers remain wage-workers — proletarians. The capitalist relation is not done away with. It is, rather, brought to a head. But, brought to a head, it topples over. State-ownership of the productive forces is not the solution of the conflict, but concealed within it are the technical conditions that form the elements of that solution." available at https://www.marxists.org/archive/marx/works/1880/soc-utop/index.htm accessed 1.2.21
See Also Bukharin, 1918, Some Fundamental Concepts of Modern Economics available at http://www.leftcom.org/en/articles/2020-08-21/bukharin-on-state-capitalism-and-imperialism accessed 17.6.21

It is just idealism to believe that capitalism can create a perfect society. What Capitalism has done is laid the basis for a new era in human society – be it an advance into socialism or a decline into barbarism

Barbarism is...?

> He (Marx) discovered that these same laws regulating the present economy, work towards its collapse, but the increasing anarchy which more and more endangers the very existence of society itself, by assembling a chain of devastating economic and political catastrophes.[83]

Marx identified the alternatives for concluding the conflict between the working class and capitalism as socialism or the common ruin of contending classes[84] and it is this mutual ruin that has since been called barbarism by socialists.

Marx's phrase of 'mutual ruin' suggests basically a collapse of productive systems and social institutions that is accompanied by the collapse of socially accepted behaviours.   It is however based on capitalism's essential competitive and confrontational nature where wars spring naturally out of economic and trade competition. But this remains quite a broad explanation.

So, can we now be more precise as to what barbarism is then?

Well, that's the real problem because nobody knows what it will be - precisely because it is just a prediction for the future.

There would seem to be various scenarios of barbarism that we can suggest:
- total catastrophe caused by atomic warfare or ecological collapse
- permanent warfare and the collapse of social structures into a society run by warlords.
- an ongoing deterioration of society ending up in another dark ages.

There is no theoretical framework to make this judgment, no real comparison in history and no writer has come up with any detailed forecasts.

The first scenario from the list above, suggests national and international conflicts could lead to an all out war that destroys humanity. Also, the relentless pace of environmental disruption by industry and politicians could simply lead to the total environmental degradation of the world and with it human society. Catastrophes such as another world war or an environmental apocalypse could destroy any capacity for human society to reemerge as a productive power (and remember without production there would be no ability for society to be anything more than a society of scavengers fighting over minimal resources).

There is little more to be discussed as these possibilities are fairly obvious and have been a feature of many books and films. I do not suggest we take the

83   Luxemburg, What is Economics in Mary Alice Walters 1970 *Rosa Luxemburg Speaks* Pathfinder Press
84   Marx & Engels, 1848, _The Communist Manifesto_ available at_ https://www.marxists.org/archive/marx/works/1848/communist-manifesto/index.htm accessed on 1.2.21

scenarios from the likes of the Mad Max films, Waterworld or the Terminator series as real, but they are forecasts based on the threats and possibilities we can all see in society - just like all science fiction stories. The threat of nuclear war is real as is the threat from environmental disaster but we cannot know just how they will show themselves in future and indeed, we cannot say definitively that some sort of human intervention cannot mitigate these issues despite capitalism's evident tendencies to make things worse.

The threat of environmental collapse is a little different in that we can definite that it has already started. We can do no better than turn to David Attenborough and his film 'A Life on Our Planet' in which he catalogues the impact humanity has had on the planet during his own lifetime. His assessment is quite simply that humanity is destroying the biosphere that maintains our life. Staggeringly wild animal life amounts to only 4% by weight of all life on the planet, whereas humanity itself accounts for 33% and the animals bred to feed us account for over 60%. The next century will be critical if we are to rescue humanity but capitalism cannot do this, only the working class can change our approach to preserve the world.

In terms of the warlordism scenario, perhaps the key point to consider is that capitalism is a competitive system at all levels of society and it encourages divisions and conflict between political parties and social groupings (ie based on race, religion, gender, locality and so forth). It would seem more likely that the increasing difficulties in the way capitalism and its economy works, will generate more and more conflict between factions in society. We can see evidence of this type of conflict in many poorer countries across the world in recent decades. From Northern Ireland and Yugoslavia to middle eastern countries such as Syria, Lebanon and Libya to African countries such as Ethiopia, Sudan and Mali we have seen countries that have collapsed into civil war and chaos or have been taken over by brutal dictators. Perhaps the present gangsterism in Columbia and Mexico should be considered relevant too. As these examples show, however, this is not a new trend in capitalist society and nor have individual situations been totally insoluble, but the question would be are we seeing more and more of this scenario? Nor is it impossible to conceive that civil wars could break out as a result of the power plays by populist politicians such as Trump, Duterte, Bolsanaro, Lukashenko. Their isolationist and self serving policies reflect the failure of mainstream politicians and economists and, if taken to an extreme, are very socially divisive.

We could look at society today and suggest that we already have barbarism. World wars and constant regional wars and the enormous death toll of the last century[85] are a sound basis for this view which, in fact, is put forward by many. It is compounded by the increasing role of the state in running society, by the enormous growth of debt in recent decades and by the inability of the ruling class to find solutions for social and economic policies that actually work to stabilise society.

---

85   See Appendix 5. The majority of the events with the largest death tolls have taken place during this last century of capitalism. Lets be clear its the capitalist society that leads to these conflicts, not everything can be blamed on bad people.

Capitalism throughout its life has always been a brutal system which cares little for high death tolls, poverty and hunger. In that respect little has changed, capitalism has always been barbaric so it seems premature to suggest that the system is already in ruins.

The scenario of a collapse into barbarism remains a forecast for which we also have little guidance. The Roman Empire collapsed and led to a period called the dark ages that could easily be called barbarism as well. This period lasted many centuries until the new structures of feudalism were able to emerge and dominate. Perhaps then barbarism could be another 'dark age' that may be permanent but maybe it could contain the possibility of a working class reaction to the chaos. In fact we just don't know how to explain what the end of capitalism will bring. Capitalism has grown and expanded rapidly, so does this mean its decline will also be fast or will that internal strength that facilitates rapid growth mean it can maintain itself for an extended period of decline? The truth is we just don't know.

Nevertheless, more and more people are becoming aware of the dangers caused by the all too evident problems in this society we live in (like the Professors Wolff and Roberts who we have seen, can detail ever worsening social and economic problems) and so in that sense confirm Marx's prognosis.

The greater awareness of these trends in society is itself a judgement, maybe even a confirmation, that what we are seeing in capitalism today is decay and a slide into barbarism. The longer capitalism goes on, the more it builds up ever greater contradictions.

As you can see, this text is avoiding drawing a firm conclusion about what is happening to capitalism at present. As is often suggested, real life is far weirder than fiction - and we are not likely to be able to accurately guess what the future has in store for us. Such questions are important in that we should have is an awareness of just how much the current trends in political, social and economic affairs are indicative of decay. It is something that we all need to take seriously and follow in world events. Forecasting will always lead to many different opinions, but what there is today is a real need to be aware of the dangers that a collapsing capitalism can bring.

Socialism is...?

As Marx demonstrated, the inherent tendencies of capitalist development, at a certain point of their maturity, necessitate the transition to a planful mode of production consciously organized by the entire working force of society in order that all of society and human civilization might not perish in the convulsions of uncontrolled anarchy[86]

Socialism is, it is true, also a forecast, a projection of what might be possible. However Marx argued that we do have an actual basis in the world we know for understanding some of what might be possible.

How on earth can we build such a society? Why do socialists say we know this can happen?

The capitalist relations of production pit the working class and the ruling class against each other in a struggle that cannot be resolved. The ruling class needs to exploit the working class to maintain its system and keep making profits. The more it can reduce the cost of labour the more profit it can make. Yet for the working class the opposite is true, to make itself better off it must fight to reduce the profit made by the ruling class. This relationship between worker and owner, between working class and ruling class, is always antagonistic. It is an unending economic conflict that plays out in the workplace but emerges sporadically into open political warfare.

The possibility of a socialist society therefore starts with this permanent class antagonism, but is also framed by what the working class actually is. It is effectively propertyless, has nothing to defend in the existing society, has no interest in taking over that exploitation and exploiting others. As all workers are equal, when the working class struggles against the exploitation it suffers, it is fighting for a free future based on the equality of all and the elimination of exploitation.

So when the working class rises up to fight the system that exploits it, when as a whole it recognises it will need to be organised and will need to take power away from the capitalist ruling class to prevent that exploitation reappearing, its power will not be based on an army or legal authorities and so forth, its power can only be based on the participation of the mass of the working class, on its unity Workers join up and organise themselves in assemblies and take unified actions to defend themselves and promote the struggle against the ruling class. Generally speaking, the more intense and political the struggle becomes, the more the working class unifies and the more powerful the workers can become and it is this tendency that provides the possibility and the desire to reorganise society to benefit all and to stop the violence of the ruling class state.[87]

---

86 Luxemburg, What is Economics in Walters 1971 *Rosa Luxemburg Speaks* Pathfinder Press

The working class is already a fully socialised or integrated productive force. The capacity of the productive apparatus means that all the world's needs could be satisfied if production were to be managed differently; a society of abundance has become possible which means money and private property are no longer either necessary or constructive. The working class' conflict with capitalist exploitation is a conflict that can bring unity to the working class and a recognition that it is a class that has real power in society. This power to band together reflects the common situation and the equality of all workers, and it is this that creates the possibility to build a new society not based on exploitation but on the common interests of humanity.

The working class experiences production as planned production for society, not as production for self, and so, if and when it succeeds in taking over society, it is going to create a world in its own image by extending its organisation, its unity and social production to all sectors of humanity.

Capitalism, by having brought all this about, has created the conditions for the working class to take over and build a socialist society. However nothing is automatic.

What can we say about what socialism[88] will be then? Some pointers would be:
-
- A socialist society must also be worldwide, it must get rid of capitalism in its entirety because capital and money are such insidious creatures they will only creep back in and take over again[89]
- It will be society which is classless, a society without nations, and without a dominant state apparatus
- Everyone will take part in working for society and everyone will be of equal status whatever their role
- It will have to be a society where everybody works in a planned economy so production and distribution will be the key factors in how society functions not exchange on an anarchic market
- It will be a moneyless society so there will be no exchange of commodities, no private property, no wages and no wage slavery
- There will be common ownership of all resources and therefore common responsibility to look after all peoples
- There will be no rich, no leaders and no bosses as it will be a society in which everyone takes part in some form in the decision-making processes through workers' councils
- There will be no state that has to use violence to control or subdue the population
- Any organisations must be organised by delegates and delegates must be mandated and immediately recallable otherwise there will be a tendency to reproduce professional leaders

---

87 Examples of such struggles are the Paris Commune in 1871 and the wave of revolutionary struggles at the end of WW1. The strike wave from the late 1960s to the early 1980s was at a much weaker level of struggle so was only a glimpse of what is possible.
88 See also the quote from Engels in Appendix 4
89 For this reason socialism in one country is impossible

- Not only will workplaces be reorganised but so will the support systems for the family, for children, for the ill, for the old and infirm
- Decisions will be made on the basis of what's best for humanity and not on the availability of money

Marx's slogan was "from each according to their ability, to each according to their need".[90]

Given the condition the world today finds itself in, there will be important tasks which will have to be undertaken in order to create socialism. It won't be socialism just because the worker class holds power, the class will have to put measures into place to reorganise life to work in a better way and some tasks will be important to start as soon as the working class takes power for example:

- Start to draw everybody in society into the working class itself and thereby over a period get rid of all classes
- Creating assemblies that will allow all workers to take part in decision making
- Write off all debts and get rid of financial institutions as the start of a process of stopping the use of money as wealth and exchange
- Plan and implement systems for managing health care and social welfare organisations but especially redirecting and reeducating them to serve people's actual needs not society's financial concerns
- Plan and implement systems for managing education organisations which will initially need to redirect them to engage all learners in a discussion and review of social needs and to engage them practically in social transformation – no doubt dependant on age though
- Maintain and organise agriculture and food supply for the whole population. This is essential to get right in the early stages of the new society
- Find ways to improve the conditions in the poorer countries of the world which have suffered the major famines and wars which have lead to mass migrations
- Find ways to redress the degradation of the environment that capitalism has caused. This means changing our diet, returning land to the wild, increasing forestry and especially rainforests
- Find ways to limit the increase in world population
- Find ways of eliminating global poverty and ensuring social development in poor regions of the world
- Plan to convert completely to sustainable energy
- Quickly eliminate harmful and waste industries especially the mass production of means of war but also the insurance and financial industries
- Start to reorganise cities and transportation systems. Bordiga suggested spreading out the big cities across the countryside but nowadays the idea of protection the countryside is likely to gain more support

---

90 Marx,1875, *Critique of the Gotha Programme available at*
    https://www.marxists.org/archive/marx/works/1875/gotha/ accessed on 1.2.21

No pressure then! Frankly this is not a comprehensive list, it is only a small portion of the tasks that will have to be undertaken.

Don't forget though that should the working class takes power, it will already have the mass of the population on its side and it will already have to skills, abilities and resources to produce whatever is needed. Its been doing that for the ruling class for the last 300 years anyway.

Let us be clear, socialism is not something that can be willed into existence, it is not a set of idealist dreams and we cannot say precisely how this society will be organised or how our behaviour will be changed.

To make up ideas as to what we want would be purely idealistic. Remember it is not our ideas that determine society but real society that provides thinkers with their ideas. A new society cannot come into being simply because some people think it possible. This is why a socialist analysis has to be based on the reality of material conditions in society and the class struggle and the possibilities they provide for the working class.

Marx was clear that socialism is the movement of the working class and what it can build - not an idealistic goal to be dreamt up in advance.

So what is not possible through forecasting is to identify exactly how socialism can be organised and exactly how humanity will behave in a society based on equality. Racism, sexism, and social prejudice in general are products of class societies based on divisions and inequalities experienced today and in the past. We know we want to get rid of these and other problems in the way people behave eg greed, prejudice, selfishness, but we cannot predetermine how we do it. By getting rid of the power of the ruling class and the domination of work over our lives, we can get rid of the alienation each worker feels against society and other people. This means we can eliminate the prejudices and conflicts that keep us isolated and antagonistic to others. We may have ideas as to what is needed – and indeed it is good to develop critiques of existing behaviours – but that cannot mean we know exactly what can emerge when the weight of the whole working class attempts to transform how society works and behaves[91]. Don't be put off by this uncertainty, the understanding of how socialism can be created should give us all confidence in the possibilities it offers.

Let's finish with one last, thought-provoking quote from Luxemburg on economics. Political economy or economics as it is known in the 21st century only exists through the domination of commodity production and private property. This does not mean the some form of accounting won't be necessary to make judgements about benefits versus costs to production. But the disappearance of private property and the accumulation of capital and wealth will mean the replacement of capitalism with a society based on social production and social ownership ie production and ownership by society as a whole not individuals.

---

91   "The philosophers have only *interpreted* the world in various ways. The point however is to *change* it" Marx, 1845, *Theses of Feuerbach* available at https://www.marxists.org/archive/marx/works/1845/theses accessed on 1.2.21

"The last chapter of economics will be the social revolution of the world proletariat" [92]

In capitalism, everything is always about money and, in the end, money and private property always gets in the way of humanity,

---

92 Luxemburg, What is Economics in Mary Alice Walters 1970 *Rosa Luxemburg Speaks* Pathfinder Press

APPENDICES

Appendix 1

Paul Frölich wrote in his biography of Luxemburg: [93]

> From a letter written by Rosa Luxemburg on 28 July 1916, from the women's military prison (*Barnimstrasse*) in Berlin to the party publisher, I.H.W. Dietz, we know the general plan of the whole work, which was to have included the following chapters:
>
> 1. What is Economics?
>
> 2. Social Labour (*Die gesellschaftliche Arbeit*).
>
> 3. Economic-Historical Perspectives: Primitive Communist Society.
>
> 4. Economic-Historical Perspectives: Feudal Economic System.
>
> 5. Economic-Historical Perspectives: Medieval Town and the Craft Guild.
>
> 6. Commodity Production
>
> 7. Wage-labour.
>
> 8. The Profit of Capital
>
> 9. The Crisis.
>
> 10. The Tendencies of Capitalist Development.
>
> In the summer of 1916 the first two chapters were ready for printing, and all the other chapters already in draft. However, only chapters 1, 3, 6, 7, and 10 could be found among her literary remains These were published in 1925 by Paul Levi, unfortunately with many errors, arbitrary alterations and the omission of important notes.

---

93   P Frohlich, 1994, *Rosa Luxemburg: Ideas in Action*, Pluto Press

Appendix 2 History of Political Economy by Rosa Luxemburg

Excerpt from: Hudis, P (ed.) (2013) The Complete Works of Rosa Luxemburg, Volume I: Economic Writings I. London: Verso Books

There is no decent book on political economy. Only a good Marxist could write a history of political economy.

The fundamental aspects are in Marx's Theories of Surplus Value. But [to read] that is very heavy going, except for the first part.

The least demanding small book that I can recommend to you as a reference work [is]: [John Kells] Ingram, History of [Political Economy]. A very superficial presentation, but useful as a reference work.

By and large, we can distinguish the following schools of political economy.

The Mercantilists

The oldest are the mercantilists. The mercantile system had already developed in the sixteenth century, with the [growing] money economy in the cities, and absolutism's great need for money. The first issue they dealt with was: "Wealth equals gold." Hence [they wrote] inquiries into the question of money.

The very titles of [the first mercantilist] writings are indicative: [Gaspero] Scaruffi, "About Money," written in 1582. The second is: [Bernardo] Davanzati, "Lectures on Money," 1588"

"Then an interesting work: Antonio Serra, "Brief Treatise Concerning the Basis on Which States Possessing No Mines Can Obtain Gold and Silver," written in 1613. This book title is typical of the mercantilists.

The primary thought content of the [mercantilists'] school is: "wealth equals gold." Their main concern: "How to bring gold into a country?" The balance of trade [was the answer]: to trade so that more was imported than exported. To pay premiums for exports and to embargo imports or impose tariffs on them.

Anyway, the [key question for the mercantilists [was]: the question of [foreign] trade.

The most important English mercantilists are:

Thomas Mun, A Discourse of Trade from England unto the East Indies, 1621

[Josiah] Child, "On Trade and Interest on Money," 1668

[William] Temple, Observations upon the United Provinces of the Netherlands, 1672

(At that time the Netherlands had come up in the world,8 and was England's biggest competitor.)

All the economists of Germany in the seventeenth and eighteenth centuries were mercantilists. But not outstanding, just parroters of the Italians.

The Physiocrats

The physiocrats were the second school. Marx dates the history of political economy from them. France is the place of their birth. They stand in sharp opposition to the mercantilists. They explain: What is wealth? Land and the soil, nature and labor. They hold that only agriculture is productive. Why? Because here labor provides more in quantity of output than labor itself costs. In contrast, trade and industry are unproductive.

At first glance this seems to be a feudal theory. In outward appearance, a purely reactionary school.

However, they draw the following conclusion: Since agriculture is the only productive branch of the economy, it is therefore fair and just that all taxes be applied to agriculture and that industry and trade be left entirely free from taxation.

In the first part of Theories of Surplus Value, Marx wrote very beautifully on this subject. Until then one could not tell whether this theory [of the physiocrats] was reactionary or revolutionary. Marx showed that with this theory the bourgeoisie made its appearance, though still under the wing of feudalism.

They [the physiocrats] demanded personal freedom and equality for the people working on the land, so that this branch of the economy could develop sufficiently for it to bear all the burdens placed upon it. Therefore a fight against feudal burdens. And thus it was a highly revolutionary school of thought.

The main founders of this school were:

"[First, Pierre Le Pesant de] Boisguilbert: 1. "Treatise on Grain and the Grain Trade."10 2. "On the Nature of Wealth, Money, and Taxes"11 He died in 1714.

Second was the official founder of this school, Fr[ancois] Quesnay, personal physician of the king [Louis XV]. He [Quesnay] lived from 1694 to 1774. His chief work is his famous Tableau Économique. In it he portrayed the society as a whole.

The book had as its motto: "Poor farmers, poor kingdom; poor kingdom, poor king."

Third: [Anne-Robert-Jacques] Turgot, finance minister under Louis XVI. His main activity was to carry out reforms and take measures that were in the spirit of this school. His chief written work was "Reflections on the Formation and Distribution of Wealth."

This school had a colossal influence on thinking people. Above all, it had a retroactive effect in relation to Italy.

The names of the most prominent Italian physiocrats, who all lived in the eighteenth century [are]: [Antonio] Genovesi, [Pietro] Verri, [Giovanni Rinaldo] Carli, [Cesare] Becarria (author of a brilliant book against the death penalty).

The German physiocrats, who lacked all significance, [included]: Karl

Friedrich Margrave of Baden. He wrote his book in French, so that Germans would not be able to learn the principles he advocated.

The Classical School

[Among the French authors in] the classical school Marx counts the physiocrats, from [MS. Illegible]16 to [Jean Charles Léonard de] Sismondi.

[Englishmen of this school were:]"

"[David] Ricardo: 1772–1823.

His main work was: His most famous pupils were John Stuart Mill and the latter's father, James Mill.

Adam Smith, 1723–90. His main work, about the "wealth of nations," appeared in 1776.

Among Smith's followers in Germany, only two became more or less well known, although they were entirely lacking in independent significance and merely parroted Smith:

Prof. [Karl Heinrich] Rau and Prof. [Heinrich von] Storch. The latter lived in St. Petersburg [in Russia], although he was a German.

Thus it may be said that until then Germany did not exist as far as political economy is concerned.

The only [German economic school] is the so-called historical school. Its founder is Professor [Wilhelm Georg Friedrich] Roscher, but Professor[s] [Bruno] Hildebrand and [Karl] Knies [were] together with him.

From the historical school, [German] Kathedersozialismus developed. It was founded in 1872 at Eisenach.

This school wants to gloss over class conflicts entirely."

"Its main representatives are: [Albert] Schäffle, [Adolph] Wagner, [Gustav von] Schönberg, all of them professors.

Kathedersozialismus has long since passed away, having been absorbed into the camp of the employers.

One of these professors even voted for the anti-socialist laws.

FURTHER READING (AN INCOMPLETE LIST)

Volume 2 of Marx's Capital.

Volume Five of the Handwörterbuch für Staatswissenschaften; the essay on crises by Prof. [Heinrich] Herkner of Zurich.

Volume 3 of Marx's Capital.

Parvus [Alexander Helphand], Aufschwung und Gewerkschaften, published in Dresden.

[Max] Schippel, Hochkonjunktur und Wirtschaftskrise.

Appendix 3

Four important definitions of economics: [94]

Economics Definitions

Adam Smith [Wealth definition]

"Economics is the study of the nature and causes of wealth of nations".

Alfred Marshall [Welfare definition]

"Economics is the study of mankind in the ordinary business of life implies that in everyday life people usually seek material well-being".

Lionel Robbins [Choice or Scarcity definition]

"Economics is the science which studies human behaviour as a relationship between ends and scarce means which have alternative uses".

Paul Samuelson [Economics of Growth and Development]

"Economics is the study of how men and society choose, with or without the use of money, to employ scarce productive resources which could have alternative uses, to produce various commodities over time and distribute them for consumption now and in the future amongst various people and groups of society".

geteconhelp.com

---

94 Geteconhelp.com, 2020, *Definitions of Economics* available at
https://geteconhelp.com/economics-definition-meaning accessed on 14.10.20

Appendix 4　Engels on the Evolution of history

This is a brief summary by Engels of the historical development of class society [95]

Let us briefly sum up our sketch of historical evolution.

I. Mediaeval Society — Individual production on a small scale. Means of production adapted for individual use; hence primitive, ungainly, petty, dwarfed in action. Production for immediate consumption, either of the producer himself or his feudal lord. Only where an excess of production over this consumption occurs is such excess offered for sale, enters into exchange. Production of commodities, therefore, only in its infancy. But already it contains within itself, in embryo, anarchy in the production of society at large.

II. Capitalist Revolution — transformation of industry, at first be means of simple cooperation and manufacture. Concentration of the means of production, hitherto scattered, into great workshops. As a consequence, their transformation from individual to social means of production — a transformation which does not, on the whole, affect the form of exchange. The old forms of appropriation remain in force. The capitalist appears. In his capacity as owner of the means of production, he also appropriates the products and turns them into commodities. Production has become a *social* act. Exchange and appropriation continue to be *individual* acts, the acts of individuals. The social product is appropriated by the individual capitalist. Fundamental contradiction, whence arise all the contradictions in which our present-day society moves, and which modern industry brings to light.

A. Severance of the producer from the means of production. Condemnation of the worker to wage-labor for life. *Antagonism between the proletariat and the bourgeoisie.*

B. Growing predominance and increasing effectiveness of the laws governing the production of commodities. Unbridled competition. *Contradiction between socialized organization in the individual factory and social anarchy in the production as a whole.*

C. On the one hand, perfecting of machinery, made by competition compulsory for each individual manufacturer, and complemented by a constantly growing displacement of labourers. *Industrial reserve-army.* On the other hand, unlimited extension of production, also compulsory under competition, for every manufacturer. On both sides, unheard-of development of productive forces, excess of supply over demand, over-production and products — excess there, of labourers, without employment and without means of existence. But these two

---

95　Engels, 1880, *Socialism - Utopian and Scientific*
　　https://www.marxists.org/archive/marx/works/1880/soc-utop/index.htm accessed on
　　1.2.21

levers of production and of social well-being are unable to work together, because the capitalist form of production prevents the productive forces from working and the products from circulating, unless they are first turned into capital — which their very superabundance prevents. The contradiction has grown into an absurdity. *The mode of production rises in rebellion against the form of exchange.*

D. Partial recognition of the social character of the productive forces forced upon the capitalists themselves. Taking over of the great institutions for production and communication, first by joint-stock companies, later in by trusts, then by the State. The bourgeoisie demonstrated to be a superfluous class. All its social functions are now performed by salaried employees.

III. Proletarian Revolution — Solution of the contradictions. The proletariat seizes the public power, and by means of this transforms the socialized means of production, slipping from the hands of the bourgeoisie, into public property. By this act, the proletariat frees the means of production from the character of capital they have thus far borne, and gives their socialized character complete freedom to work itself out. Socialized production upon a predetermined plan becomes henceforth possible. The development of production makes the existence of different classes of society thenceforth an anachronism. In proportion as anarchy in social production vanishes, the political authority of the State dies out. Man, at last the master of his own form of social organization, becomes at the same time the lord over Nature, his own master — free.

To accomplish this act of universal emancipation is the historical mission of the modern proletariat. To thoroughly comprehend the historical conditions and this the very nature of this act, to impart to the now oppressed proletarian class a full knowledge of the conditions and of the meaning of the momentous act it is called upon to accomplish, this is the task of the theoretical expression of the proletarian movement, scientific socialism.

Appendix 5

Source: White M, 2011, *The Great Big Book of Horrible Things: The Definitive Chronicle of History's 100 Worst Atrocities*, Norton

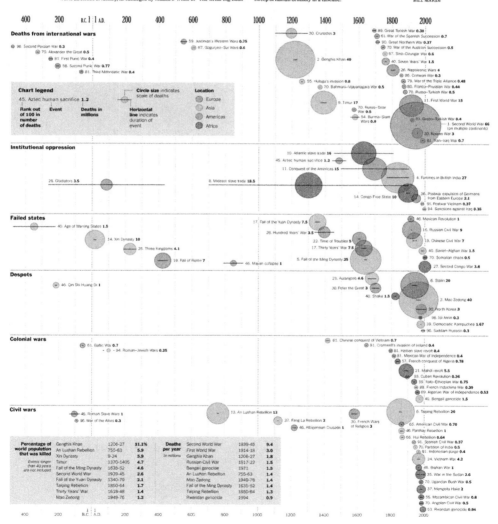

OTHER BOOKS BY THE SAME AUTHOR

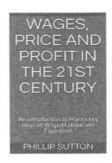

Wages, Price and Profit in the 21st Century

self-published on Amazon by Phillip Sutton

An explanation of the key concepts contained in Marx's 'Wages, Price and Profit' focusing on the basic elements of waged labour and how it creates wealth. Marx wrote his book over 150 years ago so not only is our everyday language different but also many aspects of society have changed in the meantime so it is important to bring the ideas up to date and to relate them to today's conditions.

Printed in Great Britain
by Amazon